ROBIN CHICHESTER-CLARK

ROBIN CHICHESTER-CLARK

A Passionate Moderate

NIGEL WATSON

P

PROFILE BOOKS

First published in Great Britain in 2020 by
PROFILE BOOKS LTD
29 Cloth Fair
London ECIA 7JQ
www.profilebooks.com

10 9 8 7 6 5 4 3 2 1

Printed and bound in Great Britain by Clays Ltd, Elcograf S.p.A

A CIP catalogue record for this book is available from
the British Library.

ISBN 978 1 78816 2449

Typeset in Dante by MacGuru Ltd

For Emma, Mark, Fia, Adam and Tom

C. C-C

CONTENTS

PART ONE

BEGINNINGS

CHAPTER ONE

PRELUDE

Robin Chichester-Clark was born at home at Moyola Park in County Londonderry on 10 January 1928. Although relatively modest in scale for a family which had played so prominent a part in Irish life for more than two centuries, it is a fine classical house, idyllically set, surrounded by mature woods, standing on a rise above the river Moyola, where the dollaghan, a species of sea trout unique to Lough Neagh, leap the waterfall in the garden as they make their way upstream to spawn. Robin never fell out of love with his birthplace. Although as a second son, Moyola would never be his, he visited the house regularly until almost the end of his long life. Here he found the love of nature which bound him as much as family to the land of his birth. 'Free to roam the woods, lakes and bogs at will,' his son Adam would say at Robin's memorial service, 'my father formed a deep and abiding love of the countryside and the wild creatures within it, particularly its birds.'[1]

Moyola was a tranquil refuge from the strife which had divided Ireland less than eight years before Robin was born. The border created by the Government of Ireland Act 1920 had been drawn up specifically to strengthen the position of

---

1 Adam Chichester-Clark, 'Moyola Childhood', 25 Jan 2017; footnotes are given when quotes are taken from sources other than the interviews conducted for this book, which are listed in the note on sources, p165.

Ulster's majority Unionist population. Partition and its consequences would dominate the first half of Robin's adult life. Ironically, the border was approved by the Conservative politician Walter Long, whose strongest supporter was his Parliamentary Private Secretary, the ardent Unionist Sir William Bull, lawyer, politician and grandfather of Robin's second wife, Caroline. By the time of that second marriage, Robin's political career was almost over, as extremist views on either side of Ulster's sectarian divide squeezed out the political middle ground he had occupied for so long.

As he was growing up, Robin was surrounded by reminders of his family's political inheritance. Ancestral portraits still hang on the walls of Moyola's library and dining room. Among them is Joshua Dawson; the Dawsons came to Ulster in 1633 when they acquired land nearby, and gave their name to the local village, Castledawson. Joshua was a member of the Irish Parliament and for a time Chief Secretary for Ireland. He also developed part of central Dublin, including Dawson Street, where one of the properties was accepted by the City Assembly in 1715 for £3,500 to cover his costs, an annual rent of 40 shillings (which he later waived) and a loaf of sugar. It has remained the city's Mansion House ever since. The present house at Moyola was completed in 1768. The last Dawson to live at Moyola was Mary, granddaughter of George Robert Dawson. She married Lord Adolphus Spencer Chichester, Robin's great-grandfather, in 1872.

Robert Peel, the future Prime Minister – he served two terms, in 1834–35 and 1841–46 – became George Robert Dawson's brother-in-law in 1816 when George Robert married Peel's sister Mary. By then, George Robert already knew Peel well since they had been close friends at school at Harrow. A pugnacious defender of the Protestant Union, he first served under Peel in the Irish administration in 1812. From 1815 until

1830 he was MP for County Londonderry, an area several of his descendants would later represent. He held a number of government offices, thanks largely to the influence of his brother-in-law. For much of his career, George Robert followed a conventional Unionist line, consistently opposing any relief for Ireland's Catholic population. But while he might argue in favour of the suppression of the Catholic Association as 'a wild, irresponsible and seditious assembly', he would also condemn Protestant unrest in the north of the country, writing to Peel in 1825, 'I cannot help blushing for my Orange friends; their perverseness and obstinacy is lamentable, but it really seems that there is something in an Irishman's head which prevents him from distinguishing right from wrong.' George Robert's provocative public utterances masked more moderate views personally held. His political undoing was his gradual conversion to the cause of Catholic emancipation. In the summer of 1828, his sympathetic remarks about Catholic sufferings in the past and for emancipation could scarcely have been calculated to make a greater stir, made as they were at a dinner to celebrate raising the Siege of Londonderry in 1689. As a result, George Robert fell out of favour with his brother-in-law, for whom George Robert's outburst made progress towards emancipation more difficult, and lost the confidence of the powerful Beresford family who controlled his parliamentary seat. He was unrepentant, remarking that 'several things combined to stir up a strong feeling against any moderate declaration of opinion, but which rendered it necessary at the same time for men who know more of public feeling than is to be found in such a remote district as Derry to endeavour to open the eyes of the public to the real situation of Ireland'. Nearly a century and a half later 'strong feeling' would be stirred up against the moderate opinions held by Robin Chichester-Clark, who had also striven to 'open the eyes of the public to the real situation of Ireland'.[2]

The Chichesters and the Clarks came together through the marriage of Marion Chichester, Robin's mother, to James Clark in 1922. Both families were always supporters of the Union, and for that reason, staunch defenders of partition. Robin's grandmother, Dehra, who had married into the Chichester family, sat in the newly created Stormont Parliament as the member for Londonderry.[3] One photograph in the family album shows Robin's paternal grandmother and his uncle, Francis Clark, standing outside Moyola alongside Lord Craigavon, the first Prime Minister of Northern Ireland from 1921 until his death in 1940. At Stormont, Dehra was one of Craigavon's strongest supporters. Robin and his older brother James were driven to enter politics partly by the family's tradition of civic duty; as Robin later recalled, 'the idea that we had to do something in public service was thrust upon us'. In 1955 Robin was elected as the Ulster Unionist MP for the City and County of Londonderry, holding the seat until 1974, and in 1960 his elder brother James took over his grandmother's Stormont seat, becoming the penultimate Prime Minister of

---

2 The History of Parliament, Member Biographies, George Robert Dawson, https://www.historyofparliamentonline.org/volume/1820-1832/member/dawson-george-1790-1856

3 Dehra Kerr-Fisher took her name from her birthplace, Dehra Dun, north of Delhi, India. Born in 1882, she was the daughter of James Kerr-Fisher, who owned extensive property in the USA, where Dehra was educated. She married Lt Col Robert Peel Dawson Spencer Chichester in 1901. She served in the Stormont Parliament from 1921 to 1929 and from 1933 to 1960, when she retired through ill-health. She was one of two women elected to Stormont in 1921 and the first woman to hold a ministerial post in the Northern Ireland Government. She received the OBE in 1918, the DBE in 1949 and the GBE in 1957. She died in 1963.

Northern Ireland in 1969. Robin, who was much more in love with politics and politically more ambitious than his brother, resolutely defended partition throughout his political career, although he came to believe that partition had been rushed, a hard border was a mistake and a federal arrangement would have been preferable.[4]

Craigavon believed in a Protestant government for a Protestant people and gave no ground to the minority Catholic population. The Chichester-Clarks, on the other hand, inherited George Robert Dawson's more moderate strain of Unionism. Thus, while Robin's grandmother, Dehra, was sufficiently committed to the Union to support gerrymandered political boundaries to create false majorities for Unionists in areas with a strong Catholic population, she also supported moves to improve housing, health and education for Catholics. Robin's younger sister Penelope, who as Penelope Hobhouse became well known as a garden designer and writer, never believed her grandmother 'was a hard unionist at all', while Robin felt she was 'comparatively liberal-minded'. Moyola, said Penelope, was 'one of the few Protestant estates that employed Catholics'. Religion, said Robin, had never played a major role in the family when he was growing up. 'That's been an advantage and a disadvantage … it's made it easier to deal with the problems of Northern Ireland because I wasn't brought up to hate Catholics. My family were very strongly broad-minded on that and we always employed Catholics.' The Moyola Park Association Football Club, founded in 1879–80 under the patronage of Lord Adolphus Spencer Chichester, with its ground within the boundaries of Moyola

---

4 History of Parliament Oral History Project, Robin Chichester-Clark (History of Parliament, RCC), http://www.historyofparliamentonline.org/volume/oral-history/member/Chichester-Clark-robin-1928

Park itself, has always been a non-sectarian club. The 'big house' had a certain respect locally because of the folk memories of George Robert Dawson's humanity towards local people who suffered in the Irish potato famine or the Great Hunger, as it became known. During the winter of 1846–47 starving women and children queued at Moyola's door from dawn to dusk. It was said that the bell in Moyola's rooftop belfry was rung regularly to summon villagers to the house for food. Most men, other than the oldest and weakest, noted George Robert, stayed away. 'I have been obliged', he wrote, 'to turn my kitchen into a bakery and soup shop to enable me to feed the miserable children and mothers that cannot be sent away empty. So great is their distress that they actually faint on getting food into their stomachs ... death is dealing severely and consigning many to an untimely tomb ... I see enough to make the heart sick.'[5]

Robin always had mixed feelings about his Anglo-Irish background. His sister Penelope regretted the Anglo-Irish bloodline that flowed through the family. 'We married the same sort of people all the time. And I hated that, I wished we had some Irish blood because I want to be Irish, not English. And I do think Robin did feel that, I think he did feel the same rootlessness, because we aren't really Irish, whatever we say, and we aren't really English.' Robin, said his daughter Sophia (Fia), tended to feel English in Ulster and Irish in England, contradictory feelings shared by his daughter Emma and son Mark, who, like Fia, spent their childhood in Ulster. Emma shared her father's feelings: 'I always felt weird being Anglo-Irish; I felt uncomfortable about it'. While Mark was happy with his

---

5 Parliament, RCC; letter from George Dawson quoted in *An Economic History of Ulster 1820–1939*, ed. Liam Kennedy and Philip Ollerenshaw, Manchester, 1985, p28.

Irish roots, he never much liked the description Anglo-Irish, skewering it by describing himself as 'Iro-Anguish'.

Perhaps Robin's ambivalence arose partly because, although politically he was a defender of the Union, culturally he had been brought up to think of Ireland as one country. He was influenced by his grandmother, Dehra, who had grown up with Irish history and literature, poetry and politics. At one time she was president of Ulster's Council for the Encouragement of Music and the Arts. As a boy, Robin would spend part of his summer holidays at her English home, Leigh Court, not far from Branscombe in Devon, where she lived following her second marriage to Henry Parker, a retired admiral. Sitting on the long shingle beach, Robin would listen to her reciting her favourite poetry, including Yeats, one of Irish nationalism's most passionate supporters. In its yearning for the peace and beauty of the poet's native land, 'The Lake Isle of Innisfree' was one of Robin's favourite poems. His lifelong love of poetry and literature, which also came from his mother Marion, stood him in good stead in his life post-politics when he became a successful fundraiser for the literary charity the Arvon Foundation through which he came to know Ted Hughes and Seamus Heaney. It was, he said, one of the most fulfilling times of his life.

Robin and Ted got on famously when they first met at a dinner for Arvon. Their mutual love of fishing dominated their conversation almost to the exclusion of anything else that evening. Robin and Seamus discovered they had grown up at opposite ends of the same village, Castledawson, and shared the same affection for the countryside of their youth. Robin had a great capacity for friendship. He had charm in abundance and loved people, whatever their background. He had, said his friend Alastair Colgrain, 'a very catholic disposition towards people and he had a common touch; he would talk to anybody on an equal footing and had no airs or graces at all'. 'One of the wonderful things about Robin', said his sister Penelope, 'was that he was a friend of everybody's. His gardener would come to be paid and Robin would spend two hours talking to him. He was incredibly good at talking to people of any background.' 'Shall we go down to see if the parliament is sitting?' he would ask his son Mark when he came down to stay for the weekend at Robin and Caroline's country house in the Somerset village of Yarlington. He was referring to the local pub where he loved to discuss the state of the world with his neighbours over a pint before lunch. In his last years, when he took his morning walk with his springer spaniel from his London home in one of the 'Alphabet Streets' off the Fulham Palace Road to leafy Bishop's Park, he would happily spend time leaning on his thumb-stick, chatting with whoever came along.

Robin's love of people served him well as an MP. He had the ability, said Mark, to put people at their ease. 'When we were walking round Ballymena together, when he went to get his beloved [Holland House] tobacco or had a mixture made up, he would often meet someone going out of the shop, and say, "Ah! Here's my friend!"' He would stand in the street, his arm around someone he knew, deep in conversation or sharing a funny story. The Duke of Abercorn, who as Lord Hamilton (James Hamilton) was a fellow Unionist MP during the 1960s, remembered how 'one always had a very easy relationship with Robin'. Robin, said Stratton Mills, another Unionist MP and friend, was 'always very approachable and friendly: when you ran into him in the House of Commons, he would always stop for a minute or two'. Robin made friends regardless of their politics; some of his closest friends in the House sat on the opposite side of the chamber, such as Ben Whitaker, Merlyn Rees and Ray Carter. Ray, the Labour MP for

Birmingham Northfields, first met Robin properly when they were on a parliamentary delegation to Iran in 1971, discovering he shared Robin's love of literature.

Robin found people endlessly fascinating. He loved his constituency work as an MP and never neglected his electors, earning widespread respect on both sides of the sectarian divide. He had been one of the first Ulster MPs to introduce a regular constituency surgery. (They were, he admitted, slow to take off: sitting all afternoon without a single caller, his hopes rose as an elector came through the doors, only to sink again as he discovered the purpose of the visit was to try to sell Robin a kitten.) When he stood down from his seat in 1974, the editorial in the Unionist-supporting *Londonderry Sentinel* noted that while he could be criticised for his political views, he was much admired for everything he had done on behalf of his constituents.

Robin had been talked about as one of the most promising politicians of his generation. He served as a whip in the Macmillan Government and held several front-bench posts when the Conservatives were in opposition. Disappointed to be denied ministerial office when the party returned to government in 1970, his eventual appointment as a minister in 1972 came too late. Two years later, after he had failed to find a safe Conservative seat on the mainland, his political career came to a premature end.

Ultimately Robin, as his Parliamentary Private Secretary and friend Norman Tebbit reflected, was the wrong person representing the wrong seat at the wrong time. His moderate views were drowned out by the extremists on both sides during the turmoil that engulfed Ulster. The Troubles, which began in his own constituency on 5 October 1968, wrecked his political ambitions. In the following month, when he spoke in the House of Commons about how 'the great hope of a détente between the two communities lies in the dedicated moderate opinion in Northern Ireland, which understands this problem, and which, if left to get on with the job, has both the courage and the patience to see it through', he knew in his heart that his optimism was misplaced. By the end of the year, he was predicting the imposition of direct rule over Ulster from Westminster, a move he believed would signal the end for Unionism's moderates. Their demise began sooner than he expected, in the 1970 General Election, when Ian Paisley, Robin's bête noire, defeated moderate Unionist Henry Clark in Antrim North. Robin could see that the same tide was likely to sweep him away too; he knew, as he said later, that 'the moderates in my constituency were not enough'. Moreover, his position as a member of Ulster's Unionist establishment had become a disadvantage. As Mary Holland, the *Times* columnist, observed in May 1969, 'the country landowners' influence in Unionist party politics is something which Protestant working class voters are coming increasingly to resent'.[6]

It took time for Robin to find his calling outside politics. He found that his interest in people was well suited to a career in professional recruitment while the extensive network of friends, colleagues and acquaintances he created during his time in politics and headhunting, allied to his engaging personality, made him an outstanding fundraiser for charities. David Pease, who ran the Arvon Foundation for many years, recalled that 'Robin was the most brilliant fund-raiser in the world because he knew almost everybody and he knew how to charm them all.'

While Robin relished politics and found immense satisfaction from his work as a fundraiser, it was family that became

---

6 CCLK3/8, Hansard, 4 Nov 1968; Parliament, RCC; CCLK3/26, Press Cuttings, May 1969

his priority. He always knew this although he had struggled to make it his first commitment during his years in the House of Commons. He realised he had been unable to spend as much time as he would have liked with his three older children, Emma, Mark and Fia, from his first marriage to Jane, and he was determined not to make the same mistake once he left politics behind. When he became the father of two more sons, Adam and Tom, after his marriage to Caroline, his new job allowed him to come home every evening to make up bath-time quizzes for the boys and read to them. Emma could see that her father wanted to be completely involved with them. 'He hadn't had the opportunity to do that with us because he was only half there.' He became a friend to his children as well as a father. 'All five children', said Fia, 'would say that our father was their best friend, which is quite an achievement.' Mark recalled how

> the phone would go on Sunday night and I knew it would be him. He would want to know what had been going on in our lives during the week. I still half-expect it to ring. The call would start with 'Hello Boy' or a slightly reproachful 'Where have you been?' My first reaction, still, to hearing the first curlew in March is to want to call him to tell him.

For his son Tom, Robin 'became my most trusted person', and he turned to his father with every anxiety, every concern, every secret. His brother Adam too felt able to tell his father anything. For Adam, 'there was nobody else in the world with whom I shared as much emotional or intellectual ground'. 'My father was a wonderful listener,' said Fia. 'He was very good at constantly being in touch, telephoning to check if we were OK, and he could sound quite cross if he felt we hadn't been in touch with him. He made all of us feel very loved.'

CHAPTER TWO

EARLY LIFE

Robin Chichester-Clark was the second son of James Chichester-Clark and his wife Marion. He would be their middle child, preceded by his brother James in 1923 and followed by his sister Penelope in 1929.

His father James, born in 1884, was, just like his own children, the offspring of a union between two distinguished Ulster families, the Clarks and the Lenox-Conynghams. Joining the Royal Navy in 1899, he served with distinction during the First World War at Gallipoli, Jutland and on the Baltic Mission (during which he played an important part in the 'mutiny'), winning the Distinguished Service Order and bar, the Croix de Guerre and the Légion d'Honneur. He would retire from the service with the rank of captain in 1929, when he followed the family tradition and entered politics, representing South Londonderry in the Stormont Parliament.

In 1922 he married Marion Chichester on her eighteenth birthday. Twenty years younger than her husband, Marion was the daughter of the splendidly named Robert Peel Dawson Spencer Chichester, the grandson of the Marquess of Donegall, and his wife Dehra. Robert Chichester had died in 1921 at the age of 48, after serving as the MP for South Londonderry in the UK Parliament for just 152 days, one of the shortest tenures on record. His only son, also Robert, had predeceased him in 1920, aged only 17. To continue the Chichester name, James Clark changed his surname on marriage to

Chichester-Clark. When Robin was born, he was christened Robert, taking the name of his maternal grandfather and uncle.

The turmoil that had engulfed the country prior to partition was still fresh in the minds of local people. Robin's sister Penelope was told by her mother that at one time it was not safe for anyone to walk out on the lawn on a summer's evening for fear of gunmen firing across the river. Religious divisions were never far from the surface. A succession of Ulster Presbyterian servants would tell Penelope terrifying stories of Catholic men stringing up and bayoneting dogs. Employers, she remembered, were often under pressure from their Protestant workforce not to take on Catholics.

'We had a very privileged life,' Robin recalled of his childhood. He was brought up in the nursery at Moyola Park where he and his sister were looked after by a series of nannies and governesses. His parents enjoyed winter sports, regularly travelling to Switzerland for the skiing season. One of Robin's earliest memories was travelling by train to Switzerland third-class with his nanny and nursemaid while his parents went first-class. He also recalled his father taking him by the hand and helping him fill a pail with fallen acorns from the vast oak trees around the house to feed to the pigs in the farmyard. There were visits to maiden aunts, Charlotte and Alice Lenox-Conyngham, at the Manor House, Moneymore, County Londonderry, near their ancestral home, Springhill. Alice had been a passenger on the maiden voyage of the *Titanic* but only on the first leg, disembarking at Cherbourg. They were affectionately known as 'The Trumpets' from their use of ear trumpets as hearing aids. Robin would recount how he could tell what they had consumed for lunch by the stray peas and carrots which found their way into the trumpets. When the trumpets squealed, the dogs howled.

An early family photograph album offers glimpses of Robin's childhood. It is filled with touching images of Robin, known as 'Tink' in the family, with his siblings. In the summer of 1929, not yet two years old, Robin appears as a little blond boy in a smock, white socks and sandals. One photograph shows Robin and his brother James holding hands with their father, all three in their swimming costumes, with Robin looking up fondly at his father. Two years later the same scene is repeated, except that this time it is Robin and Penelope holding hands with their father. Every photograph of the children is set outdoors, showing the boys fishing or swimming, skiing or playing tennis. They are often surrounded by dogs, usually labradors or spaniels, for which Robin developed a lifelong love.

Robin was soon robbed of his father. When James Chichester-Clark travelled to Switzerland as usual in the winter of 1933, he was suffering from a heavy cold, contracted after a day shooting duck at Shane's Castle, immersed up to his waist in cold water in Lough Neagh. In Switzerland the heavy cold became pneumonia, and in an era before antibiotics this proved fatal. He died at the Palace Hotel in Gstaad on 31 January 1933. His death had a profound effect on an uncomprehending five-year-old Robin.

The body of Robin's father was brought back from Switzerland and on the bleak February day of the funeral, Robin and Penelope were playing in the nursery. 'The blinds were drawn down on the windows which reached nearly to the floor,' Robin wrote many years later. 'Nanny and the nursemaid, crouching by them, stealthily raised the blinds from time to time to note the arrival of those coming from Largantogher[1] who called first at the house on their way to the graveyard at

---

1 Largantogher was the Clark family home near Maghera

the end of the front drive.' Later the same day, his uncle, his father's brother, Francis Clark, came up to the nursery to tell the children they had lost their father. All Robin could think about as his uncle picked him up and hugged him was how prickly his chin was.[2]

> We children were, I know, aware that something momentous had happened; speaking for myself, I was sure it had something to do with my father. It was the first time in my life that I had felt that lingering, perplexed and unanalysed anxiety, common enough as one grows up … the nursery was very quiet all day save for the sound of gravel churning as the cars turned on the sweep outside the front door.[3]

His father's death was never mentioned: there was, Robin later said, 'a kind of notion that you did not allude to the dead for fear of arousing sadness and embarrassment'. Robin often went with his mother to lay flowers on his father's grave: 'I did not ask questions and nothing in particular was volunteered.' The refusal to discuss it left Robin unable to grieve for his father; instead, his head was filled with imaginings about the horrors of death's decay. His mother was obliged to view the corpse of anyone on the estate who died, which she hated, and Robin recalled stories of eyes weighted down by coins, chins propped up by prayer books and faces turning green. When Robin knew a dead body was lying in the gate lodge, he cycled the long way round to and from the village to avoid passing by.

---

2 Parliament, RCC

3 Robin Chichester-Clark, Personal Papers, 'Moyola Childhood', n d: further quotes relating to Robin's childhood in this chapter are taken from this source

For a few years after his father's death, Robin's life became routine once again, although by now James had been sent away to prep school in England. Robin's mother would play with Robin and Penelope each evening in the nursery before Nanny put them to bed. From County Wicklow, Nanny was a much-loved and benevolent influence on the children. One of her favourite sayings was, 'Is it nice, is it kind, is it necessary?' Nanny frowned on talking after lights out, threatening to run away with the local police constable, although she always relented after the children pleaded with her. One much-loved nursemaid, Pearl, sometimes crept into the nursery to read the children a story but her successor, Sadie, was apt to use the strap on their bare legs more frequently than seemed necessary.

Summer holidays were often spent at the seaside village of Castlerock, five miles west of Coleraine. Much advance planning was required. An old blue lorry from the estate carried a jumble of belongings the 35 miles to the coast. Among them were Nanny's sewing machine, wind-up gramophone, window boxes and caged canary. The family stayed for three or four weeks at the Villa Marina, 'a white house with green shutters, [with] a commanding view of the village in front and mostly grey sea at the back'. Whenever possible, the children played on the windswept beach, warned not to go near the treacherous bar mouth where the River Bann entered the Atlantic. Childhood summers, Robin remembered, were never warm and sunny; at Castlerock, 'the weather was consistently diabolical'. Gales came with thunderstorms that left Nanny terrified.

In a storm, she cried to Pearl to pull down the blinds and threw herself under the bed as the heavens challenged. We were all pressed into her bedroom where, to please Nanny,

Pearl would leave her shelter to wind the gramophone, for Nanny was obsessed then with a recording of a ship sinking in a storm to the sound of howling winds and splintering timbers while its passengers gave a fearful rendering of 'Nearer my God to Thee'. It all seemed perfectly normal.

Then, when Robin was nearly seven and his sister five, things took a turn for the worse. Beloved Nanny retired, replaced by Mitzi Mauch, a Swiss-German governess, described by Robin as 'a plain, manly-looking woman [who] showed little feeling for us'. The daily routine for these two small children was one of exercise, education and eating. After rising early for breakfast, Robin and Penelope were hastened onto the front lawn where they wielded Indian clubs. 'We vaulted, turned somersaults, squatted on our haunches, hands on hips, with arms and unwilling legs made to shoot out like Cossack dancers and, as a finale, tried to stand on our heads.' Education was elementary instruction in English, French and maths. Long, tiring walks were a regular feature of each afternoon. As for eating, 'we were stuffed with food: bread and butter, slice after slice; two helpings of the dreaded rennet and rice puddings, or tapioca, until we feared mealtimes. We groaned with food.' It was Penelope who suffered most, Mitzi taking a dislike to her, keeping her at the table for hours until she finished her food or attempting to speed things up by forcing spoonfuls down her throat. 'When Penny had finished retching, she was sometimes compelled to stay where she was until she had sampled her own vomit.' Robin felt he should have been able to protect his sister but simply did not know at that age how he could.

The two siblings became closer as a result of these shared experiences. 'Robin and I did a huge amount together,' said Penelope, 'because we were near the same age.' There was plenty of rough-and-tumble sibling rivalry. Just as James made sure Robin knew he was the leader of the pack, so Robin tried to assert his superiority over his sister, although she quickly learned to put a stop to any intimidation by screaming loudly. 'We had this most wonderful river,' Penelope recalled, 'and nobody cared that we couldn't swim and we just took a boat and went out. We had a very wonderful free life in that way; we were spoilt because we could really do what we liked.'

In September 1936 Robin was sent at the age of eight to Selwyn House, the prep school in Broadstairs on the Kentish coast that his brother James had just left. For Robin, it was the happiest part of his early education. He found he was inclined towards the humanities, which he enjoyed, and that he was good at sport. He would leave the school as head boy. 'Nevertheless, there was nothing like getting home. Arrival to a rush of friendly dogs, then indoors to see such guinea pigs as two energetic red setters had spared, out again to see a collection of rare and not so rare bantams provided by a generous Aunt Eleanor.' (Eleanor Clark was the sister of Robin's father.) Moyola offered a rich playground: 'We wandered, my siblings and I, among apple and pear trees, sometimes sampling cherries from the garden walls. With Barnacle Bill, a favourite black cocker spaniel, who was expertly prising fruit from low hanging stems, we worked our way through the raspberry canes.' Robin loved the river, the hills and the bogs surrounding Moyola. He worshipped his older brother, often acting as his cartridge bag carrier, striving hard to keep up with him as they strode across the bogs looking for snipe.

But then came Dartmouth. The question for Robin's mother was what to do with her second son. Since James, then at Eton, was expected to return and manage the estate, what was Robin to do? Marion, who had married a diplomat, Charles Brackenbury, in 1938, decided Robin might follow his father into the Navy. After all, said his mother, Robin with his rolling gait would be well suited to life on the open sea. In 1941, at the age of 13, he was sent as a junior cadet to the Royal Naval College at Dartmouth.

It could hardly have been a more inappropriate choice. Opened in 1905, the impressively massive College buildings were clearly intended to convey the imperial majesty and might of the Royal Navy, then at the height of its power. But in their imperious, impersonal and aloof detachment, they were everything that Robin was not. 'It was a total disaster,' recalled Robin. 'I hated every minute of it, I shouldn't have been there, I didn't do very well there.'[4] Robin was never practical and as a sensitive boy his failings left him feeling miserable and humiliated. When it was Robin's turn to raise the flag on the parade ground in front of the whole school, he would pull the wrong rope and the flag would fall forlornly to the ground. While sailing, having just gone about, Robin made the mistake of picking up the cap knocked off the officer's head and using it as a bailer, for which he earned a serious reprimand. He hated the practical curriculum which was devoid of any culture and his lack of aptitude for maths contributed to his failure to pass out. His mother was unimpressed by her son's lack of success, which compounded Robin's misery. The irony was that his brother James, originally destined to return home after Eton, had joined the army as soon as war was declared and would become an outstanding soldier. His only consolation was the opportunity for bird-watching in the nearby woods.

For Robin, the one saving grace was the evacuation of the College to the Cheshire countryside after the buildings in Dartmouth were bombed in September 1942. The College moved to the grounds of Eaton Hall, the country seat of the Dukes

---

4 Parliament, RCC

of Westminster, where the cadets were housed in Nissen huts in the surrounding parkland. (Later, Robin would become friends with his fellow Unionist MP, Robert 'Pud' Grosvenor. When Pud succeeded his brother to become the 5th Duke of Westminster in 1967, Robin and his second wife Caroline stayed with Pud and his wife Viola in the new house they built on the site of the previous Victorian Gothic mansion.)

In wartime returning home from school across the Irish Sea was risky, given the threat of German U-boats, and naval vessels escorted Robin's ferry. Home life was disrupted too. The main house at Moyola was requisitioned by the army in 1940, first for a succession of different British regiments, latterly for the US 82nd Airborne Brigade, which left the house when the invasion of Europe began in 1944. During those years the family lived in the cottage in the grounds.

It was probably Robin's uncle, Francis Clark, who suggested his nephew might apply for a place at Cambridge as he did to Robin's sister Penelope. Educated at Rugby and Cambridge, Francis had been ordained, serving as a curate at St Mary the Great in Cambridge before spending his career as a don at his own college, Magdalene, where he was chaplain and taught history. Francis, recalled Penelope, 'was our guardian. During the war he was sent to teach at Eton where they called him "God", and he was rather like God. He was a lovely, lovely man.' He became the fatherly influence in Robin's life and it was a blow to him when Francis died suddenly during an operation in 1953.

Robin's first step towards Cambridge was attending a crammer in Norfolk to gain his qualification in Latin, essential for university entrance, which had not been taught at Dartmouth. He went up to Cambridge at the age of 18 in the autumn of 1946 with a place at his uncle's college. Looking back, Robin always felt he had been too young. This feeling of immaturity convinced him that he had in fact only been 17 when he went up. Many of his peers, returning from wartime service, were much more mature. For Robin, Cambridge represented freedom from the straitjacket of Dartmouth's severe discipline, opening up, he soon discovered, 'a vista of women and wine and that kind of thing'. Robin was always short of money and on one occasion asked his brother James for a loan to pay his railway fare home. James refused, telling his brother to pawn his fishing rod instead, which Robin did, although he later managed to scrape together the cash to get it back. Studying first history and then law, he made sure he did enough work to get through his exams, usually working through the night, sustained by copious amounts of black coffee. But, as he later reflected, it was a time when he thought 'life was for living'. He recalled his law tutor telling him, 'You're a nice boy, Chichester-Clark, but you don't do any work,' although Robin's work ethic was hardly helped by his tutor's practice of taking his reading groups off to Devon so he could indulge his passion for fly fishing on the county's classic spate rivers. Robin would always regret his preference for racing at Newmarket over Pevsner's lectures.[5]

Robin made many friends, including the Kabaka of Buganda, who was with him at Magdalene. Popularly known as Freddie, the Kabaka was, recollected Robin, always beautifully dressed and spoke the most elegant English, but he failed every one of his history exams. Their paths would cross again during the 1960s, when Robin was part of a delegation tasked with helping Freddie to overcome the political problems he had with the newly independent Ugandan Government. Freddie's difficulties remained unresolved and he fled into exile in England, where he died in 1969.

---

5 Parliament, RCC

Although Robin joined every one of the university's political associations, a sign of his interest, he was never active. He did, however, speak once at the Union. In 1948 one of the Union's guest speakers was Éamon de Valera. He had just lost his outright majority in the Dáil for the first time since 1933. Leaving the conduct of opposition politics to his deputy, Seán Lemass, de Valera embarked on a worldwide tour to win support for the dismantling of partition. One of Robin's friends, from south of the border, invited him to sit next to the great man at lunch. They got on very well, said Robin, discussing everything except politics. But Robin found himself in such disagreement with de Valera's argument when he heard him speak at the debate that evening that he got up to say so. De Valera, said Robin, was 'amazed to find that the person sitting next to him at lunch was rather opposed to his views'.[6]

Robin and Penelope saw a lot of each other at Cambridge when Penelope came up to read economics at Girton in 1948. The university had finally granted women the right to take degrees but, as Robin recalled, 'they were still looked down on and they had to push themselves quite hard to get recognised'.[7] One of Penelope's friends was Jane Goddard, coming up to Girton to read English. The daughter of a distinguished RAF commander, Air Marshal Sir Victor Goddard, Jane was travelling with a friend on the train to Cambridge when they spied another girl joining the carriage, carrying in one hand a lacrosse stick, tennis racquet and fencing foil, and in the other a large basket filled with books. 'We looked at her with a certain amount of horror,' said Jane. The same girl was soon knocking on Jane's door in college – it was Penelope Chichester-Clark. 'We immediately became friends,' said Jane.

---

6 Parliament, RCC
7 Parliament, RCC

Within a week Jane knew that Penelope had a brother at Magdalene. Penelope told her that Robin had asked her to find some girls to bring along to a party. Penelope, Jane and another friend cycled to Robin's digs where they found several other young men but not Robin. He only turned up later, looking somewhat exhausted, having played rugby the day before in London (he was a playing member of the London-Irish club) followed by what was obviously a good night out. Jane and Robin soon became friends and she invited him along to the Christmas Ball at Girton. Jane was already developing her love of music, which she also encouraged in Robin, but she may have been too earnest that evening in taking him away from all the fun to listen to a recording of a Brahms piano concerto on her record player. Robin, said Jane, 'really floated through Cambridge'. He was in the company of young men whom Jane in her earnestness considered lightweight and she felt at the time that she wasn't really on the same wavelength as Robin. There was no romance. 'He was very attractive and amusing and fun but I would never have dreamt of falling in love with him.' Robin himself had several girlfriends and he would often bring tales of heartbreak to Jane.

One of them concerned a distant relation, Rosemary Chichester, who had decided to turn Robin down in favour of John Brooke, the son of Basil Brooke, the Prime Minister of Northern Ireland. Robin had spent some time with Rosemary during the summer of 1949 when he had flown out to the USA to spend several weeks staying with his mother and stepfather on Long Island. At the time Charles Brackenbury was serving with the United Nations in New York. Robin was keen to see more of the country and raised funds by working as a coffee boy at Time Inc, where he was known to everyone as Bert Clark. He remembered people worrying about taking on a graduate to make coffee. They 'thought it very odd that someone with a degree should be involved in this sort of thing,' said Robin, 'and they said, "Don't you think this will be socially damaging?"'[8]

His travels took him hitch-hiking halfway across the country to Kansas. He stayed just south of Kansas City with Don Casement, an elderly relative of his grandmother's. Robin remembered how Don and his partner drank glasses filled with equal parts of gin and sherry in the evenings. He took part in a round-up, the first time in years he had been on a horse. (He never really liked horses: when he was a boy, a pony called Richard he was riding at Moyola not only threw him off but bit him on the arm when he tried to get up again.) He was warned to stay in the saddle since the ground was riddled with venomous copperhead snakes.

Robin's experience at *Time* magazine helped him to make up his mind when he returned to the UK that he would like to take up journalism. His first step towards working in Fleet Street, he was told, should be to take a post with a provincial newspaper. He joined the *Portsmouth Evening News*, eventually becoming features editor of the *Hampshire Telegraph*, where he enjoyed adding new sections to the paper. But he became jaundiced about the national press when a visiting reporter from one of the big dailies made up a completely fictitious interview after failing to meet his intended interviewee. On the other hand, Robin felt in retrospect that the time he spent talking to people from every background, learning all about their lives, did help him in his political career. Learning to ask the right question to elicit what he wanted to know came in useful during his time as a whip.

While he was in Portsmouth, Robin lived in lodgings, the walls of his bedroom covered in many different photographs

---

8 Parliament, RCC

of the grave of his landlady's husband. He didn't eat well when he was there and his poor diet contributed towards an ulcer which led him to leave the paper and spend time convalescing at his beloved Moyola. While he was recovering, a friend suggested he might like to consider the new post of press and publicity officer being advertised for John Christie's well-established opera house at Glyndebourne in Sussex. Robin's musical education had been only partially completed at Cambridge and he knew little about opera but he decided to do some research and sent in an application. He got the job and enjoyed it hugely, wining and dining a constant stream of music critics while developing a deep and lasting love of opera. In 1952, for example, with others from Glyndebourne, he was involved in staging two performances at St Pancras Town Hall of Mozart's *The Impresario*, Holst's *Savitri* and Menotti's *The Telephone*, providing a young Colin Davis with one of his first chances to conduct opera.

At Glyndebourne Robin discovered that Jane Goddard was a member of the chorus. She had decided to concentrate on a career in music, joining Glyndebourne from the London Opera School after taking singing lessons with renowned baritone Roy Henderson.

> Robin decided that he was very strongly attracted to me, he decided he was in love. That made the whole thing quite different because then I had to take him much more seriously and wonder what I really did think about him, and I wasn't sure at all what to do because I really wasn't completely in love with him in the same way.

Jane decided she had to get away. Through the British Council she arranged to spend eight months in Vienna, which was still divided between the British, Americans, French and Russians.

Jane took singing lessons with the teacher of the famous soprano Sena Jurinac, whom she had always admired.

After a month she concluded that her relationship with Robin wouldn't work. She wrote to Robin telling him so. 'I felt very happy and free, I'd done it, it was all right.' But a week later she was called to the phone by her landlady. Robin was on the end of the line. He claimed to have decided as he was on his way to visit his mother in Geneva that he would stop over in Vienna to see her. Given how difficult the journey was, and how hard it was to get into the city, Robin's decision must have been made much earlier. Jane could not help admiring his determination. Would she, asked Robin, come down to see him for he was already at the station? They spent a week together in Vienna. Jane agreed to think about marrying Robin but insisted on completing her singing lessons in Vienna. Eventually, she returned to England. 'Robin met me off the boat at Dover and drove me back to London and we became engaged.' It was Coronation Year, 1953, and by then Robin was working in London for the Publisher of the Oxford University Press: John, later Sir John, Brown, popularly known as 'Bruno'. Jane was introduced to Robin's mother Marion, who had taken a flat for the Coronation, and the two women would form a close and affectionate relationship. Robin's sister Penelope, recently married to Paul Hobhouse, returned from her honeymoon to hear that her brother had become engaged to her friend. 'I couldn't believe it,' she confessed, 'I couldn't believe it.' She simply didn't believe that her brother was in love.

Matters did not proceed auspiciously. Robin, said Jane, wanted only a small wedding, and she eventually found Chelsea Old Church, where one chapel was still in use following the wartime bombing of the church. 'My father and mother were horrified; they wanted to have a big wedding for me. My mother wanted me walking down the aisle in white with lots of bridesmaids. And Robin said, no, sorry, can't do that.' Only family were invited to attend. 'My mother was so disillusioned that she said it didn't matter what I wore, I might as well wear my grey coat and skirt, but Penny, my dear sister-in-law, said we can't have that and took me off to a rather nice couturier in Sloane Street and got him to make a rather attractive dress which I wore.' The couple were married on 6 November 1953. Two weeks later Jane's parents held a large reception at the Apothecaries' Hall, inviting all the friends they had wanted to come to the wedding.

The young publisher and his soprano bride began their married life in a second-floor flat in Eccleston Square. While they were living there, their first child, Emma, was born in St George's Hospital, Hyde Park Corner, in 1955. The couple would have two more children, Mark, born in 1957, and Sophia, born in 1961, but by then the Chichester-Clarks were in Northern Ireland.

PART TWO

THE POLITICIAN

CHAPTER THREE

THE COMING MAN

In 1954 Robin Chichester-Clark was selected to succeed William Wellwood as the Ulster Unionist candidate for the City and County of Londonderry constituency at Westminster. Although he was only 26 years old, Robin had been contemplating entry into politics for some time. He had always been interested, which was hardly surprising, given his family's involvement in Ulster politics. A sense of duty played its part in his decision, as he later recalled: 'I thought I would like to do it because my family have always done things like that.'[1] 'I was very pleased for him,' remembered his wife Jane, 'but I didn't really know what it would involve at all.'

'My grandmother', said Robin, 'was one of the biggest influences of my life.' As well as her cultural influence over her second grandson, she was politically influential. Robin remembered helping Dehra on the campaign trail from a young age and while he was at university he was occasionally asked to stand in for her as a platform speaker. She had a formidable reputation, developed over many years since she first joined Unionist politics to fight against Home Rule. She opened her first Orange Hall in 1909, helped to form the Ulster Women's Unionist Council in 1911 and organised nursing units for Carson's Ulster Volunteer Force in 1912. Awarded an OBE for wartime service in 1918, she represented Londonderry at

---

1 Parliament, RCC

Stormont from 1921 until 1929 and South Londonderry from 1933 until her retirement through ill-health in 1960. She held ministerial office at Stormont twice, first from 1937 to 1944, second from 1949 (when she was made a dame) to 1957. She prized loyalty to Ulster above all else, which made her ceaselessly critical of nationalists and independent Unionists. This led her to spearhead the fight against the system of proportional representation governing the province's local elections after partition. She was not alone in arguing that since Catholics looked to Rome and Dublin, their disloyalty disqualified them from governing in the province, even in parts of Ulster where they were in the majority. She also claimed that nationalist councils discriminated against Protestant Unionists. Stormont abolished proportional representation and redrew ward boundaries. Dame Dehra's local council in Magherafelt went from a nationalist majority of 17 seats to 11 in 1921 to a Unionist majority of 18 to 11 after 1924. On the other hand, she was willing to improve the material circumstances of Catholics as well as Protestants, believing that economic prosperity and well-being in the north, by comparison with the much lower standard of living south of the border, would help to create a greater affinity with the province and the Union among the Catholic population. Although she lacked rapport with the Protestant working class, and was scornful of fundamentalist Protestants, she enjoyed great respect among many Unionists. On her death in 1963, Jack Sayer, later an outstanding editor of the liberal *Belfast Telegraph*, and a friend of Robin, wrote to him in praise of his grandmother. 'How fortunate you are in having such an example in public life – and how unfortunate for Northern Ireland that we do not have more like her.'[2]

---

2 Parliament, RCC; Robin Chichester-Clark Papers (CCLK), Churchill Archive Centre, Cambridge, CCLK1/6

With Dame Dehra's encouragement, Robin had kept an eye on the Londonderry seat for a couple of years, knowing the incumbent was likely to stand down. Initially, he had dismissed the idea out of respect for his brother; Robin was always conscious of his status as the second son. Everything came to the eldest boy and Robin regarded the family tradition of a seat at Westminster as the preserve of his brother James. James, however, was still in the army. For Dame Dehra, no doubt it was unthinkable that the family should pass up the opportunity of filling a vacancy in the local constituency.

There was only one other local candidate when the time came for nominations but, given Robin's family background and political connections, he stood little chance. Although Robin confessed that he was 'far too young', and lacked any experience of local government, his big advantage, he said, was that 'I knew a lot of people in the area because of my grandmother who was still in politics'.[3] As Jane quickly realised, 'the Chichester-Clark name was very potent in the Northern Irish Unionist world'. This was still an era in Ulster politics when a significant factor in the selection of parliamentary candidates was, as *The Irish Times* put it a little later, 'this kind of family tradition – seen in many constituencies and often with a "big house" in the background'.[4] But this sort of establishment Unionism, epitomised by the province's long-serving Prime Minister, Viscount Brookeborough, was on the way out. A divide was opening up in Unionist ranks between the old order, represented by the landed gentry, and the new, represented by the growing urban middle classes with their interests in business and commerce.

'Getting elected was easy,' Robin later remembered. In the

3 Parliament, RCC
4 CCLK6/11

1955 General Election he won 64 per cent of the vote on a turnout of 78 per cent. After Paul Channon, Robin, just 27, was the youngest MP in the House. Most of his majority came from the Unionist stronghold of Coleraine. He held the seat continuously until he stepped down at the General Election in 1974, achieving more than half of all the votes cast at each election. By 1970, however, Robin's last election, fought in very different circumstances, his share had dipped to 53 per cent. Politics and public life effectively dominated the first half of Robin's working life. He was soon identified as a young politician to watch. In an era when the Ulster Unionist party was linked closely with the Conservative party, Robin made steady progress. Winning minor office in the Macmillan Government and holding several front-bench posts in opposition, he was widely expected to be given ministerial office when the Conservatives returned to government in 1970. That he was not, and had to wait a further two years for preferment, was one of the signs that the political world he had entered had changed irrevocably as far as Northern Ireland was concerned.

In 1955 Robin's only opponent was in prison. Marcus Canning, a local man, was standing for Sinn Féin. After the count Robin had been shown one of the rejected ballot papers: opposite Canning's name the voter had written 'Awful'; opposite Robin's, he had written 'Worse'. Canning, a member of the Derry Unit of the Irish Republican Army (IRA), had been jailed for eight years following his role in a raid on an army training school in England. This was part of the IRA's strategy to win a mandate for a renewed terrorist campaign. All 12 Ulster constituencies were contested by Sinn Féin candidates, half of them, like Canning, in jail. Two of them won their seats although they were both later removed by petitions, gifting them to the Unionists. This relative success led to the

IRA's Operation Harvest, a campaign of attacks on police and military targets, which lasted more than six years. It was brought to an end thanks to help from the Irish Government and the concerted efforts of the police on both sides of the border. The local police had advised Robin to carry a revolver in the glovebox of his car although he never did. Sixteen men were killed during the campaign, which lost the IRA support, and it was called off in 1962. But it was another reminder of the festering divisions within Ulster society. Canning stood again in 1959, winning even fewer votes than in 1955 because of popular discontent with the IRA campaign. In 1964 Robin won nearly two-thirds of the vote against his opponent, Hugh McAteer, a former IRA Chief of Staff, who stood on a Republican abstentionist platform.

'Much of the antagonism between the two communities was based on preconceived notions of the other,' wrote one historian of this period in Ulster's history. Each side charged the other with discrimination, but with nationalists controlling only 11 of the province's 73 local authorities, it was the nationalist community that suffered most. There was an uneasy peace, with each side convinced the other was wrong, but with neither on the whole prepared to take extreme action. As the same historian commented, 'Any attempt to change or challenge the foundations of these divisions could destabilise the very basis on which the citizens of Northern Ireland's polarised community could live in relative peace with one another.' As Robin himself once put it, speaking in the House of Commons in 1968, 'The wounds of Ulster are as deep as they are old and they cannot be healed overnight.'[5]

After Robin's election, he and Jane continued to live in

5 *A History of Northern Ireland 1920–1996*, Thomas Hennessy, p110 and p120; CCLK3/8, Hansard, 4 Nov 1968

London, buying a small house in Bywater Street. But with
Robin returning late every night from the Commons and then
flying off to his constituency at the weekend, they decided –
wrongly as it turned out – that they would probably see more
of each other if they lived in Northern Ireland. For the first
few years they made their home in the three-bedroom cottage
in the grounds at Moyola. As it had been for Robin, it was an
idyllic place to bring up young children. Among his daughter
Emma's earliest memories are walks with her father through
the beautiful beech woods – 'Now tell me about your life!' he
would say – and watching him fish for salmon under the waterfall. 'He was a very good fisherman,' said his son Mark, 'and he
had very beautiful casting style … it was lovely to watch.'

By the time Robin's brother James returned to the estate
from the army in 1960, the cottage was becoming too small,
particularly since Jane was expecting their third child, Fia, who
was born in the following year. Jane began looking for some-
where else they could live. It had to be affordable and close to
the airport. She found a well-proportioned eighteenth-cen-
tury farmhouse, Ross House, with some land attached, near
the village of Kells in County Antrim. Robin had little money
of his own. As the second son, he was unlikely to benefit
from the family estate in future; any money he might inherit
depended upon Dame Dehra. She took financial advice from
a distant cousin of the family, Terence O'Neill, then an up-
and-coming Ulster Unionist politician whom she mentored.
'She was a very wealthy woman,' said Robin's wife Jane, 'and
she could never quite decide what to do with her money, and
how to leave it, and as a younger son himself [Terence] would
endlessly advise her to leave it equally to her three grandchildren, but she never did, she left it all to James.' In addition,
parliamentary pay was poor, a subject of growing com-
plaints among many MPs, some of whom found themselves

in genuine financial hardship by the early 1960s. It was only through a loan – not a gift – from Dame Dehra that Robin was able to buy Ross House. Even then, he had to sell the land surrounding the house. 'He was always frightened of money,' said Emma. 'He was phobic, I think. He would forget to give my mother any money before he left after the weekend. But he wasn't interested in money either, which was his trouble.' Yet as one of Robin's rare diary entries, made in 1967, shows, a lack of money did worry him, and he was conscious he should be doing more to provide for his family. 'I am selfish,' he wrote on 9 February 1967, 'because I know that I ought to be making money for my family.'[6]

In 1961, two months after Fia's birth, the family moved into Ross House, which Jane had decorated and furnished. Although the house was in a beautiful rural setting, it was remote, reached from the nearest road down a long potholed lane; some weekends Emma and Mark could be found filling in the potholes. Simply travelling to meet friends was at least a 40-minute drive, Emma remembered. Jane loved the house but it was distant from the cultural opportunities she enjoyed so much. As she pointed out for a newspaper profile in 1963, 'If I wanted to take up singing professionally again it would be impossible to do it from here.' She began putting on plays for the children in one of the barns at Ross House. The head-mistress of Cambridge House School, a girls' school in Bally-mena, came to a performance and afterwards invited Jane to teach English at the school, which she did part-time for four years, finding it very rewarding. She also joined the Ulster Singers in Belfast, taking part in performances of works such as Stravinsky's *Symphony of Psalms* and Britten's *War Requiem*.[7]

---

6 Personal Papers, Diary Jottings for 1967
7 CLK6/11

Even so, with Robin in Westminster most of each week, and consumed by constituency matters most weekends, it could be lonely. Jane resented the Government's refusal at the time to cover the cost of flights to and from London for the wives of Northern Ireland MPs. It was easier for the wives of English MPs to feel part of their husbands' careers and she felt she missed out on the excitement filling Robin's life at Westminster. Moreover, she was one of the few English wives of a Unionist MP, most of them being native to Ulster. She knew that a parliamentary lifestyle took its toll on marriages. 'It was a very unfortunate way of living, spending Monday to Friday by yourself in a country that wasn't your own country; it may have been part of the United Kingdom but it was a foreign country in many ways.' Robin was sensitive to these concerns. He understood that for Jane, without any local connections, being in Ulster without him during the week 'was pretty maddening for her'. He was also conscious that constituency meetings and other events scarcely made things any better at weekends.

Yet there were many happy times. The family looked forward to Robin's arrival home every Friday evening. (It was Emma's favourite day of the week because it was the day her father came home and also because the local baker's van delivered her *Diana* comic.) He would sometimes bring back gifts, like avocados, in scarce supply in Ulster, and the latest Beatles single for Emma. When Robin had the time, he and Jane would enliven the weekends with pranks and games. 'He was always one for a joke,' said Mark, 'and he could be quite risqué.' They used to dress up to play tricks on the children. The doorbell would ring, and on opening the door, the children would find standing there an extraordinary couple, a peculiar old woman dressed in clothes remarkably similar to their mother's (this would be Robin) and a tall thin man

(Jane), who would ask if they could come in for a cup of tea. Once Robin and Jane suddenly appeared in the sitting room at Ross House, Jane dressed as a bridegroom, Robin as a bride, both convulsed as they performed this pantomime, Robin putting on a falsetto voice. 'He was excellent at putting on voices,' said Emma, 'and could be quite theatrical.' For a time he read regularly to the children every weekend, relishing the many different voices required, for example, by Kipling's *The Jungle Book*; 'but we weren't very good at listening, or seemed to be easily distracted, or longed to go and do something else,' said Emma, 'and the routine broke down.' He would tell wonderful stories, full of drama, humour and tension, about foxes, badgers and other wildlife, which he did for his grandchildren many years later as they balanced on his knee in the house at Yarlington.

As a young Unionist politician, Robin Chichester-Clark embraced traditional Unionism. It was an integral part of his upbringing on both sides of his family. Part of that tradition was joining organisations like the Orange Order, the Royal Black Institution and the Apprentice Boys of Derry. Being an Orangeman was considered an essential requirement for anyone seeking nomination as the Unionist candidate for a rural constituency. Robin himself had joined when he was 18: 'I was drafted in unresisting; this was expected of the son of a former Grand Master, politician and of the "big house".' The Order helped to bridge the gap between gentry and workers. 'In those days,' Robin wrote, 'class was very clearly defined and indeed in Northern Ireland there was as yet virtually no middle class. Fraternal greetings in the Lodge overcame reservations as well as some of the deference maintained elsewhere.' Robin felt that by bringing men together, the Order 'seemed to impose a restraint of silence on even the worst

sort of individuals', a view shared by a promising young politician, Brian Faulkner, from Ulster's growing middle class. As
well as restraining the more extremist Protestant Unionists,
the Order, Faulkner wrote in his memoirs, taught the value of
justice and respect for the beliefs of others. As Ulster's politics
became more extreme, this would change, as Robin would
experience personally.[8]

Unionist MPs were expected to attend the meetings and
celebrations of all these organisations in their constituencies.
Robin's wife Jane recalled

> how I had to unfurl Orange banners, and every meeting
> took place in an Orange hall, and Robin would have to put
> on his bowler hat and his sash and walk in all the proces-
> sions … but it was something he had to do in order to be
> the Unionist MP: he had to be an Orangeman, and he had
> to be a Blackman in Derry, and he had to be an Apprentice
> Boy. It was something that no English MP would be able
> to understand.

In his early years as an MP, when he was attending so many
loyalist meetings, Robin's speeches reflect the influence of
his grandmother. Addressing a large crowd gathered for the
dedication of instruments and unfurling of flags of the newly
formed Eglinton Accordion Band in June 1959, he declared
how

> in Northern Ireland we still recognise the old values, things
> like faith and loyalty. The people will eventually come back
> to our way of thinking, to value the older things which
> we uphold. We here have no need of 'angry young men'

---

8 Personal Papers, Notes on the Orange Order

because there is nothing to be ashamed of in the way our fathers and grandfathers conducted things in Northern Ireland.[9]

As a constitutionalist, he favoured the status quo in the absence of any democratic decision by the majority of the electorate in support of change, which to him seemed highly unlikely. As he told a constituency gathering in 1961, reported the *Derry Standard*, the border existed 'because there were deep differences of opinion and outlook between the people of the North and the people of the South, and 40 years had not changed or lessened those differences'. Although privately he believed partition had been implemented too hastily at the expense of community cohesion, he was robust in its defence. The Republican Labour MP Gerry Fitt came under fire from Robin for his opposition to partition in 1968. He was, said Robin, 'a good deal less interested in civil rights and good community relations than in using every weapon to hand to end partition'. He criticised 'foolish talk of a united Ireland' and attacked the Republic's repeated claims on territory in the north for stoking fear among the Protestant majority. Robin always said he would work with whichever party would retain partition and he turned down a later invitation to establish the Conservative party in the province on the grounds he had no intention of splitting the partitionist vote after spending 20 years in its defence.[10]

Robin also shared the prevalent Unionist belief that the best way to persuade the Catholic minority to accept the existence of Northern Ireland was to improve their economic

9 CCLK6/10, *Derry Standard*, 2 June 1959
10 CCLK6/10, *Derry Standard*, 22 Aug 1961; CCLK3/8, Hansard, 4 Nov 1968; CCLK1/10, miscellaneous papers, 1970–72

well-being; like many others, he worked hard to encourage greater inward investment in Ulster at a time when the mainland economy was flourishing. But at this stage in his career he failed to appreciate that what Catholics really wanted was an end to the discrimination that blighted their daily lives. Robin never held sectarian views: as a man without strong religious convictions, he was baffled at the knee-jerk hostility of each community towards the other. He could never understand the opposition from both communities to the idea of integrated education. Nor could he understand the opposition of some Protestants to his campaign to bring more international companies to Ulster on the grounds that it would benefit Catholics most. Yet while he acknowledged the discrimination against the minority in employment and housing, he argued that employers and housing authorities were understandably reluctant to confer the benefits of scarce housing or jobs on people they suspected of being sympathetic to those seeking a united Ireland, the disappearance of Ulster and an end to Unionist influence. He indicated the many other reasons apart from discrimination that might affect the employment of Catholics and pointed out that most Catholics were employed by Protestants. He attacked the ignorance and insensitivity of those who spoke of half a century of Unionist misrule: 'they had never lived in a country where a proportion of its people actually challenged its right to exist and it was not easy for them to imagine the fears and distrust of change of the majority'.[11]

Robin defended the convention that the UK Government did not interfere in matters devolved to Northern Ireland and that such matters were not discussed in the UK Parliament. The Government of Ireland Act 1920 had handed over

11 *The Irish News*, 1 May 1970

to Stormont responsibility for most of the powers that else-where in the UK were exercised by Westminster. In fact, the act made it quite clear that ultimately Stormont was subordinate to Westminster. Opposition MPs at Westminster became increasingly resentful that Unionist MPs, so closely tied to the Conservative party, could vote, for instance, on local government issues affecting England, Scotland and Wales, while they had no say on similar matters affecting Northern Ireland. It was unsurprising that the practice crumbled after the election of a Labour Government in 1964, as backbenchers with a strong Irish Catholic electorate insisted on raising the issue of Ulster whenever they could. When Gerry Fitt became the first nationalist MP to take an active part in Westminster politics, this breach of the convention was reinforced. Robin, however, continued to defend non-intervention, latterly, as violence began to break out in the province, out of concern that the UK Government would ultimately impose direct rule. Privately, he was frustrated that the convention limited his ability as a Westminster MP to influence what went on in Ulster.

He was also frustrated by the way the convention impaired the working relationship between Unionist MPs at Stormont and those at Westminster. With devolved powers not extended to any other part of the United Kingdom until the advent of Scottish devolution, the Northern Ireland Government and its backbenchers jealously guarded their special status. This, believed many of Stormont's Unionist MPs, placed them above their colleagues at Westminster. In 1956 Robin felt compelled to write to one of his Stormont colleagues, asking him to stop making unjustified public attacks on Unionist MPs at Westminster. He tried hard to develop an effective relationship between the two sides, working closely with Bill Craig after the latter's appointment as government Chief Whip at

Stormont in 1962. 'At the moment,' Robin wrote to Craig in July 1962, 'the rivalry between [Stormont and Westminster] and the buck-passing which both sides are indulging in is doing immense harm.' Neither side proved receptive. In the following year, when Robin suggested it would be beneficial if Northern Ireland ministers met their UK counterparts from time to time, this too fell on deaf ears.[12]

He was equally frustrated by the way the UK Government was happy to use the convention to wash its hands of any interest in Northern Ireland. As a former head of the Northern Ireland Civil Service, Kenneth Bloomfield, wrote, for years successive governments, 'unassisted by the radar of any effective local representation, had peered at Northern Ireland, if at all, as through a dense fog'. Robin was appalled by the attitude of Harold Macmillan which he experienced at a luncheon party attended by Unionist MPs. Their host was R A Butler, who as Home Secretary had notional responsibility for Northern Ireland. It was one of the sops flung in the Unionists' direction by the Conservative party as a means of ensuring their continued loyalty in the voting lobbies. Robin overheard one of his colleagues, Knox Cunningham, ask the Prime Minister what he intended to do about the IRA's latest bombing campaign. 'Well,' said Macmillan, 'I'll look into that but those bombs are good for loyalty, aren't they?' Robin's friend James Hamilton, Unionist MP for Fermanagh and South Tyrone from 1964 to 1970, found that until the eruption of violence in the province in the late 1960s most people on the mainland were happy to be ignorant of and ignore Northern Ireland.[13]

---

12 CCLK1/5, RCC to Bill Craig, 17 Jul 1962
13 *A Tragedy of Errors: The Government and Misgovernment of Northern Ireland*, Kenneth Bloomfield, p15; Parliament, RCC

On the other hand, given the self-imposed constraints of the convention, Robin believed that the fortress mentality of too many of his Unionist colleagues at Westminster made them unwilling to gain any understanding of the wider Union and beyond. 'We were all so local, nobody travelled,' he remembered. 'That strip of water is responsible for a lot of the trouble: nobody travelled, nobody saw things outside, all they knew was their own little Ulster ... we were just too parochial.' On entering the House of Commons, Robin wanted to show people outside Northern Ireland that there were Ulstermen with a broader hinterland. While Robin characterised some of his fellow Unionist MPs as former colonial mandarins seeking something to do in their retirement – he was probably thinking of Sir David Campbell, a previous lieutenant governor of Malta – others he described as inward-looking and simply not up to the job. As he later reflected, 'I felt, I suppose, rather arrogantly, rather critical of the people who did come into politics in Northern Ireland in those days ... I wanted to show that we could produce people from there who would take a wider interest in the world.' Robin always insisted he was British first and an Ulsterman second, which some people who had never been outside the province found difficult to comprehend. Robin himself was hardly typical. Although he came from the Unionist establishment, he had travelled further and experienced more by the time he was elected an MP than a number of his colleagues.[14]

As a group, the dozen Ulster Unionist MPs at Westminster lacked cohesion. Their political strategy was largely confined to the defence of traditional Unionist positions. For the more politically aware Unionist MPs, such as Robin, eager to play a full part in the House of Commons, the party's ties with the

14 Parliament, RCC

Conservatives gave them a way of breaking free from their Unionist straitjacket. This close relationship had existed since partition and was valued by politicians like Brian Faulkner because they saw the Conservatives as the only party that had stood constantly by Ulster's side. For Robin, frustrated by the parochial boundaries of Unionist politics, these ties gave him an outlet for his political ambition. The two sides, said Kenneth Bloomfield, were 'sister parties'. Many Unionist MPs, he wrote, were 'the sorts of people who – with different birthplaces and accents – might well have sought Conservative seats in Surbiton or Guildford'.[15] As James Hamilton recalled, Unionist MPs 'were as one' with the Conservatives, receiving whips' notices every week, 'which we followed with acquiescence'. Unionist MPs even attended meetings of the party's backbench organisation, the 1922 Committee, and one of them, Robin's friend Stratton Mills, MP for North Belfast from 1959, became a member of the Committee's executive. When Robin was first elected, he soon joined some of his newly elected Conservative counterparts in forming a discussion group which invited ministers along as guest speakers.

Within a year of his election, however, Robin's political allegiance was sorely tried by the Suez crisis. The conspiracy between the British, French and Israelis which led to the invasion of the Suez Canal Zone at the end of October 1956, following the nationalisation of the canal by the Egyptian leader Gamal Abdel Nasser, created a political crisis in the UK, damaged relations with the United States and fatally damaged the career of the Prime Minister, Anthony Eden, who resigned in the following year. The debacle had a huge impact on the young Robin Chichester-Clark. He remembered it vividly more than half a century later.

---

15 *A Tragedy of Errors*, Kenneth Bloomfield, p17

I was 27 when [the Suez crisis] happened. I was pretty horrified by what had happened. Most of us were terribly uneasy about it. It was very distressing. In those days I suppose we were all more 'empire minded' or something like that. ... I've always been very pro-American and the idea that we were upsetting the Americans to the extent that they did what they did was very foreign to me. I remember particularly one evening going home after the House had risen and getting back to my house in Chelsea, I was on my own, and I remember sitting down and for want of anything else to do – I'll never forget this, because I feel funny whenever I hear it again – I turned on Strauss's *Four Last Songs*, and within seconds ... I was actually shedding tears: this is the end of empire, we can't do anything, there'll be Soviet submarines in the Mediterranean. It was an enormous adjustment in everyone's life.

He seriously considered voting against the Government but was dissuaded from doing so by the Chief Whip, Ted Heath. This was probably the start of the friendship between the two men, which lasted the rest of their lives in spite of occasional political differences over Northern Ireland. For the music-loving Chief Whip, discovering Robin had worked at Glyndebourne, Robin was a person after his own heart. For Robin, Ted Heath 'was one of the most honest men in politics'. He recalled his refusal to provide the Conservative MP Nigel Nicolson with any assurance that the Eden Government had not been involved in deception, which led Nicolson to abstain in the eventual vote of confidence.[16]

Suez did nothing to diminish Robin's growing love of politics. He threw himself wholeheartedly into political life, to

---

16 Parliament, RCC

the extent, said Stratton Mills, that he 'gave too much of his life to politics'. 'Robin adored Westminster,' said his wife Jane. 'It was his life.' As one of the most able of Unionist MPs – Conservative party officials in the 1950s were scathing about the general calibre of Ulster Unionist candidates and MPs – Robin was identified for preferment early on. Latterly Unionist MPs had been chosen to fill the occasional position as Parliamentary Private Secretaries (PPSs), the bottom rung of the patronage ladder. James Hamilton's predecessor in Fermanagh and South Tyrone, Lord Robert Grosvenor, was PPS to the Foreign Secretary from 1957 until 1959, and Knox Cunningham's appointment as PPS to the Prime Minister followed in 1959. The last Unionist MP to hold ministerial office had been Terence O'Neill's uncle, Hugh O'Neill, later Lord Rathcavan, but once again only in a junior position, as Parliamentary Under-Secretary of State in the India Office, and only briefly, for one year in 1939–40.

It was probably Ted Heath in his role as Chief Whip who identified Robin's political potential. In 1958 Robin joined Robert Grosvenor among the unpaid ranks of Parliamentary Private Secretaries on his appointment as PPS to the Financial Secretary to the Treasury Jocelyn Simon. 'The news of Mr Chichester-Clark's appointment,' reported the *Belfast Telegraph*, 'was received yesterday with much pleasure in his constituency.' Robin, however, later confessed that 'finance wasn't my scene really'. He was much happier in the whips' office where he became a junior whip in the summer of 1960. 'Although his ambition was restrained, hidden under the bedclothes,' said Stratton Mills, 'Robin was consciously moving himself up the ladder, willing to give his life to politics.' Robin knew, as he later said, that being a whip was 'very often a stepping stone for people'. The *Belfast Telegraph* believed his appointment confirmed the expectations of those who believed Robin would sooner rather than later assume leadership of the Ulster Unionists at Westminster.[17]

'Westminster became Robin's playground,' said his wife Jane. 'He was at the heart of it in the whips' office, he knew everything that was going on, and it became absolutely his life, slightly to the detriment of his life at home, because he was always pretty exhausted.' Robin's persuasive charm – and his fondness for harmless gossip – made him an ideal whip, a role he continued to fulfil until the defeat of the Conservative Government in 1964. By then, he was a senior whip, having been made Comptroller of Her Majesty's Household in 1961. Known as White Stick in Waiting, from the accessory that came with it, this was a ceremonial post involving certain duties on royal occasions. Robin loved it and he developed a great admiration for the Queen. He relished the secrecy surrounding the world of the whips' office, attending private backbench meetings to gauge attitudes and spot trouble, collecting information on other MPs, all noted down in the whips' black book. Stratton Mills recalled Robin asking him to sit close by a Commons committee room in 1963 where a number of Tory backbenchers were holding a meeting to oppose membership of the Common Market; Robin wanted Stratton to note down every MP who came and went. 'You got to know so much of what was going on about a great many subjects,' said Robin, 'and also about the private lives of people that you became more and more secretive. You learned an awful lot about things, you learned an awful lot about human nature.' When a vote was called, and MPs had to be tracked down, Robin sometimes found himself telephoning their lovers. A note from the Chief Whip, Martin Redmayne, who succeeded Ted Heath in 1959, observed that 'The trouble

17 Parliament, RCC; CCLK6/9, Press Cuttings 1958–74

about being in the Whips' Office is, as one of you said to me, that "you have to believe honestly things which you know to be untrue". This is a wearing business ...' Robin, on the contrary, never found being a whip wearing, and he delighted in discovering the eccentricities of his fellow MPs. On one occasion, asked to whip MPs into the House for a vote, he called Lord Lambton at home only to be told by his butler that his lordship was in the bath and could not be disturbed.[18]

By convention, whips never spoke in the House of Commons, but for Robin this was not a drawback. He never really enjoyed public speaking and he made relatively few high-profile speeches outside the House until the situation in Northern Ireland became more serious. Robin, recalled Stratton Mills, 'very rarely let his views come above the parapet'. He had 'a conspiratorial nature' and he came to realise that he could be more effective exercising his influence behind the scenes. He had an agile mind and with his intimate knowledge of what was going on, it is unsurprising that he had Terence O'Neill calling him on most weekends, particularly after Terence became Northern Ireland's Prime Minister in 1963. Robin's position, and his growing political stature, also allowed him to influence the direction of political travel in the province in discussions with leading Northern Ireland politicians, like Terence O'Neill, Bill Craig and his own brother James. James Hamilton, who shared a London flat with Robin in the 1960s, remembered the frequent phone calls between Robin and Terence and between Robin and Ted Heath, who used Robin to keep him up to date with events in the province.

Robin delighted in the need to be secretive, which carried over into his private life. 'He loved secrets,' said his daughter Emma. 'He loved us to confide in him, he loved thinking he

---

18 Parliament, RCC; CCLK1/5, Redmayne to RCC, 11 Aug 1960

was the only person who knew and he loved pretending you were the only person he had told.' 'He did like to know all your secrets,' said his daughter Fia, 'and he certainly knew all mine.' On the one hand, this created an immensely strong bond of trust between Robin and his children. On the other, as Robin confessed, it wasn't a healthy habit, keeping secrets from one's wife, and this took its toll, combined with the long hours whips were expected to keep. Robin made several friends among his fellow whips, all of them Conservative MPs, notably Willie Whitelaw. One evening, sitting together in the smoking room of the House of Commons, surveying the other occupants, they asked each other whom they would have as weekend guests. Robin recalled that 'having run through the ranks of the living, they could only agree on the Labour radical Nye Bevan – who was beyond the reach of any invitation, having died the previous year'.[19]

Shortly before the defeat of the Conservatives in the 1964 General Election, Robin was invited by the US State Department to tour the country. With Jane, he travelled from San Francisco to Little Rock, Arkansas, from Chicago and Philadelphia to New York. He flew to San Francisco a week ahead of Jane in July to attend the Republican National Convention which nominated Barry Goldwater to run against Lyndon Johnson in that year's presidential election. It was a rowdy and unruly affair, with Goldwater's conservative politics splitting the party, and it must have reinforced Robin's steadfast belief in moderation and opposition to extremism of any sort. These views will have been affirmed by the visit Robin and Jane paid to Little Rock, Arkansas, where they went to a newspaper run by the black community. In shaking

---

19 *Splendid! Splendid! The Authorized Biography of Willie Whitelaw*, Mark Garnett and Ian Aitken, p53

hands with the staff, Robin and Jane did what many whites in the state still refused to do. At a dinner given for them by a wealthy white family, the Chichester-Clarks' questions on racial problems visibly irritated their hosts. Robin and Jane also observed the election campaign between the incumbent Democrat governor, the notoriously racist Orval Faubus, and his liberal Republican rival, Winthrop Rockefeller, committed to racial equality. Rockefeller would lose but go on to win the governor's mansion at the next election. For Robin, it highlighted how extremism could be found on both sides of the political divide.

After the October 1964 General Election, Robin accepted Alec Douglas-Home's invitation to become Chief Opposition Spokesman on Northern Ireland, another sign of Robin's growing prominence. The appointment did not pass without comment: the *Irish Independent* wondered whether the presence of an Ulster Unionist on the opposition front benches might cause difficulties when Northern Ireland matters were raised.

At the same time Ted Heath took over the Treasury brief, cementing his position as favourite to take over the party leadership. Robin had recognised Ted's ability many years previously. The first time Ted came to stay with Robin, Jane and their family in 1959, Robin organised an invitation to lunch for both of them with Northern Ireland's Prime Minister, Lord Brookeborough. Ted spent a week with the family in the cottage at Moyola and Robin took him into the Republic, where Ted bought some Irish tweed. Robin did not, as Ted wrote in his memoirs, smuggle him across the border under a blanket in the back of the car. What took Jane Chichester-Clark aback was Ted's lack of interest in what was going on in the province and his failure to seek out even one Roman Catholic. Robin was disappointed in later years by what he regarded as Ted's failure to understand Northern Ireland despite all the advice he gave him. While this would not have surprised him from any number of other mainland politicians, it was something he did not expect from Ted. By the time Ted came over for a second time, the family had moved to Ross House. Terence O'Neill had sent over specially his own upright piano, which was identical to the one in the Chichester-Clarks' dining room. The instruments were placed on either side of the fireplace and after lunch Ted played two-piano pieces with another guest, Viola Grosvenor, herself a very fine pianist. Ted's last visit to Ross House took place in 1965, the year in which he became leader of the party. The Grosvenors invited Robin, Jane and Ted to stay with them at Ely Lodge, their home in County Fermanagh. On this occasion Ted played the accompaniment for Jane as she sang soprano arias from Mozart's operas. It was during this stay that the guests and their hosts took a boat out onto Lough Erne, where they were marooned for a while after the engine broke down.

Ted was the favourite to win the Conservatives' first formal leadership election, following the resignation of Alec Douglas-Home. Unionist MPs were entitled to vote and Robin was part of the inner circle of MPs working to secure Ted's election. Stratton Mills recalled Robin taking him as an admirer of Ted's on the Sunday night following Douglas-Home's departure to Peter Walker's London flat where a small group was meeting to plan Ted's campaign. To avoid the prying eyes of the press, Ted and his close friend Anthony Barber came along the roof from a neighbouring property to join the meeting. Robin was asked to use his charm to drum up support for Ted among other MPs, including his 12 Unionist colleagues, eight of whom decided to vote for Ted. On election day, 27 July 1965, Robin acted as Ted's polling agent, when he was impressed by the accuracy with which Ted had forecast the result. Ted comfortably beat off his major rival, Reginald Maudling, winning more than half the votes in a three-horse race (the third-placed candidate being Enoch Powell).

In the autumn of 1965 Ted asked Robin to become Spokesman for Public Building and Works and for the Arts in addition to his front-bench responsibilities for Northern Ireland. Although these posts were outside the Shadow Cabinet, they were, reported the *Belfast News Letter*, the first time an Ulster Unionist MP had held multiple front-bench roles. Here was another sign of Robin's continuing political progress. He was particularly enthusiastic about his arts brief. One of his criticisms of the Macmillan Government had been its lack of encouragement of the arts. 'We should do more to encourage the arts both at schools and at the universities ... If we continue to talk about doubling the standard of living, we must not neglect the use of leisure,' he wrote to the Chief Whip, Martin Redmayne, in August 1960. On the election of the Labour Government in 1964, Harold Wilson had been inspired in making Jennie Lee the first ever Minister for the Arts. She was an enthusiastic advocate for the arts, helping to establish the Open University and expanding the role of the Arts Council. The Conservative party was slow to catch up and Robin was given the task of devising a strategy to match Labour's. It was on his initiative that an arts policy group was formed for this purpose in 1967 with Robin as chairman. The arts had become a political topic as a result of the spending committed by Labour but once the Conservatives had adopted their own policy, Robin wrote in January 1968, 'we will have cancelled out Labour's advantage'. Robin expected hostility to the idea from within the party, having noted on the first meeting of the group in 1967 that 'many members of the party were opposed to giving money to the arts'. It was in this role that he helped to break up the rings operated

TOP: Dehra Chichester, Marion and James and Mrs Clark on the steps of Moyola following the marriage of Robin's parents, 10 May 1922
BOTTOM: Portraits of Robin's parents

TOP LEFT: Robin's father MIDDLE: Robin's mother TOP RIGHT: Robin's uncle, Frances Clark, Chaplain of Magdalene College Cambridge BOTTOM LEFT: Robin's father at Moyola BOTTOM RIGHT: Robin's brother James, his sister Penelope, his father and Robin himself

Moyola Park

TOP: Robin, James and Penelope BOTTOM LEFT: Robin with his sister Penelope, dogs and piglet BOTTOM RIGHT: Penelope and Robin with corn stook at Moyola

OPPOSITE TOP LEFT: Robin as a naval cadet at Dartmouth, aged 13 OPPOSITE TOP RIGHT: Jane, Robin's first wife, in Maine, 1947 OPPOSITE MIDDLE: Silver Strand, Glencolmcille, County Donegal OPPOSITE BOTTOM: Ross House

top: The young Member of Parliament for Londonderry bottom: Prime Minister Harold Macmillan and government whips, 1959

TOP: Jane, Emma, Edward Heath and Robin at Connor Church by Kells, County Antrim BOTTOM: DUP leader Ian Paisley in full flow

TOP: Street scene in Northern Ireland BOTTOM LEFT: Robin in the Concorde prototype at Filton, Bristol with PPS Norman Tebbit in the background, 1972 BOTTOM RIGHT: Robin learning how to drive a digger at the Bircham Newton Training Centre, Norfolk

by corrupt antique dealers and antiquarian booksellers, an achievement of which he was very proud.[20]

The group's secretary was the young Chris Patten, who was then working for the Conservative Research Department. Robin gathered some illustrious individuals to join the group, a foretaste of his later success in the charity sector. Among them were the chairman of the Royal Opera House, the principal of the Royal College of Art, a former director of the V&A and Dame Ruth Railton, the founder of the National Youth Orchestra. Robin had resisted the suggested appointment of Peter Donald, a theatre impresario, with some justification. In August 1967 Chris Patten sent Robin a note, in which he described how Donald 'has continued on his philistine way. He is threatening to use three of his theatres [Theatre Royal, Newcastle; Opera House, Manchester; and the Royal Court, Liverpool] for three months of the year as bingo halls ... Your initial reaction to him was clearly most perceptive.'

Robin's diary entries for 1967 offer a glimpse of the opportunities his arts post gave him. When Jane joined him in London for a week in February, they went to see Claude Lelouch's film, *Un Homme et Une Femme*, and attended a reception at the Tate Gallery. 'Jane was delighted with Henry Moore,' Robin wrote, 'who was embracing everyone he met, including her.' At the end of the same month, he went with members of the Arts Amenities Committee to inspect the redecoration of Admiralty House and the Banqueting Hall. 'I can't think why I have never been to see the Rubens ceiling and the beauties of the Banqueting Hall before. It ought to be used more for public occasions.'[21]

20 CCLK1/5, RCC to Martin Redmayne, Aug 1960; CCLK 2/3, Conservative Arts Policy Group
21 Personal Papers, Selected Diary Entries, 1967–68

The diary entries suggest Robin was not entirely happy with his responsibilities at the time. Partly, this was because he felt he should be giving more time to his family, where strains with Jane were beginning to show. Partly, it was because he was increasingly involved behind the scenes in pressing the case for Terence O'Neill's reform programme in Northern Ireland. He felt he could not give the attention to his responsibility for the arts which it deserved, partly because of his other commitments, while the cost of attending all the exhibitions, concerts and other events the job entailed was becoming a financial burden. In January 1968 he gave up his role as front-bench Spokesman for the Arts at his own request. Paul Channon, who had joined the Commons at the same time as Robin in 1955, took over the post. In May Robin also ceded the role as chairman of the policy group to Channon although he continued to be a member.

CHAPTER FOUR

THE FIGHT FOR REFORM

From childhood Robin was aware of the divisions afflicting society in Northern Ireland. It was something he accepted and took for granted when he was young; it was the way things were. Growing up, as someone without a strong religious faith, he could see the rights and wrongs on both sides of the divide. When he became an MP, the composition of his own constituency brought home to him the challenges facing a society divided between two communities, each with completely different aspirations, one looking south, the other looking across the sea. Although he remained consistent in his defence of partition and the interests of his supporters, he became critical of a long-embedded culture which, he said, effectively created 'two separate societies'.[1]

Robin envied the political efforts being made in Europe to unite peoples across borders. His enthusiasm was not universally shared by his fellow Unionist MPs. Quite a number of them were hostile to the idea of being absorbed within a Catholic continent and, in the days before the Republic gained a reputation as a tiger economy, fearful of an influx of people from south of the border seeking work. Robin, who was a delegate to the Western European Union and the Council of Europe, attending meetings in Strasbourg and serving for five years on each, consistently supported Britain's attempts

---

1 CCLK3/6 Part 2, Copy of speech, c 1967

to enter the Common Market, believing that Europe was moving in a direction Ireland seemed incapable of following. The contrast must have seemed so much starker at the time Robin was writing an article for regional newspapers in 1972, when the UK was on the verge of gaining membership yet men, women and children were being blown up in Ulster because of seemingly irreconcilable differences between the two communities.

> While men in Europe, and perhaps other parts of the world, move slowly but inexorably towards a realisation that they are interdependent and indeed not vastly different in vice and virtue, those in the two parts of Ireland will, I suspect, continue to retain at best their traditional suspicions of each other until the last vestiges of geographically based nationalism in Europe have elsewhere vanished.[2]

Ten years earlier, in the early 1960s, Robin was pressing for a new Prime Minister in Northern Ireland, dismayed by the inertia of a Stormont Government led by a man blind to the need for change. Robin discussed ways Brookeborough could be persuaded to leave office with Bill Craig, who was Brookeborough's Chief Whip. According to Robin, Craig had also reached the conclusion that it was time for Brookeborough to go, backed up perhaps by what he may have learned from other Unionist MPs at Stormont. Brookeborough proved stubborn but eventually seized the excuse of a stay in hospital to announce his retirement as Prime Minister, although he would remain in Stormont for five more years, unhelpfully harrying his successor, Terence O'Neill, from time to time.

---

2 CCLK3/4, text of article appearing in *East Anglian Daily Times*, 17 Mar 1972

Robin always found it difficult to understand Brookeborough's overt hostility to Catholics. As he wrote some years later, 'I have no strong feelings about Roman Catholicism (I can, I think, point to my own record which has made me so unpopular in the majority community of Ulster to prove the point).' The Chichester-Clark household may have supported the Union but it was never anti-Catholic. James and Robin were certainly never anti-Catholic, as Robin's sister-in-law Moyra recalled. She herself came from a similar background and could never comprehend the sectarianism that plagued the province. James's blindness to religious differences, she felt, had been reinforced during his wartime service in the Irish Guards. Robin's sons recalled how their father always cheered for Ireland during international rugby matches as a team representing the whole of Ireland.

That so many Unionists were oblivious to the pressing need for change, Robin believed, arose partly from the length of time they had been in power. One consequence, he felt, was that 'everyone got lazier and lazier'. The party never undertook any of its own policy research, relying instead on the Civil Service to come up with initiatives, and even then, these might never see the light of day if they offended local interests. The party was interested only in re-election, fighting election after election almost exclusively in defence of partition, while the calibre of members returned to Stormont was often second-rate. As Kenneth Bloomfield put it, 'the Unionist benches were too largely made up of small men, whose small talent and small experience exactly matched their narrow sympathies'. They seemed incapable of tackling what Bloomfield called 'the deep and dangerous schism in [Ulster's] community life'.[3]

---

3 CCLK3/14 Correspondence on Northern Ireland, 1969–73; Parliament, RCC; *Stormont in Crisis: A Memoir, Kenneth Bloomfield*, p65, p71

Both Robin and James were hopeful that Brookeborough's successor would bring change. The new Prime Minister was Robin's close friend Terence O'Neill, who regarded Robin as his closest political advisor. They spoke most weekends when Robin was back from Westminster; Jane was often exasperated at the lengthy phone calls Robin received from Terence which interrupted long-planned weekend dinner parties. 'The coffee grew cold', Robin wrote, 'as the matter of voting rights in local government was batted back and forth in the fevered political climate of the time.' They both favoured change in key areas although they were rather hazier about what exactly that would entail. Robin's son Mark recalled how frustrating it was for a young boy whose father had just returned home for the weekend that Terence 'would turn up on Saturday mornings and monopolise [Robin] for three or four hours in his sitting room. He would come so many weekends, actually, he was there a lot.'[4] (If Robin wanted to curtail one of his lengthy meetings with Terence, he primed his children to run round to ring the doorbell at the front of the house, allowing him to announce he had more visitors to see.)

Terence, however, was politically handicapped from the moment he took office. No one voted for him to become Prime Minister; he was invited to fill the post by Northern Ireland's Governor, Lord Wakehurst. Although he was a long-serving MP and had held senior Cabinet posts, he was not a conspicuous figure at Stormont. His position was weakened from the outset by his lack of any political power base. While he was a humane and intelligent man, he was intolerant of those less able than himself and his shyness made him appear distant and aloof to those who did not know him, making it difficult for him to forge alliances with his colleagues.

---

4 Personal Papers, Terence O'Neill's Resignation

Moreover, he was seen as a member of the Anglo-Irish establishment, which worked against him since he was perceived as being out of touch with rank-and-file Unionists, who were already being wooed by Ian Paisley. All these factors, personal and political, made the role of Prime Minister more difficult than it might have been, and he would become more reliant on his friendship with Robin.

Both Robin and Terence believed reform could come only gradually. This was the only way, they believed, that it would win support from Unionist voters. Other like-minded Unionists, including Stratton Mills and James Hamilton, backed O'Neill's modest, moderate path. It soon became apparent, however, that Terence was going to take much longer to implement change than anticipated by Robin and those who thought like him.

It did not help that O'Neill appeared happier to deal in gesture politics than in concrete reform. Many Unionists howled, for example, at O'Neill's visit to a Catholic convent and were outraged by his decision to invite Seán Lemass, the Irish Taoiseach, for talks in Belfast and by his own reciprocal visit to Dublin early in 1965. More often than not Terence did nothing to prepare the ground for these initiatives with his party. James Chichester-Clark never enjoyed the same rapport with Terence as Robin but Terence had nevertheless appointed him as his Chief Whip. James found it incredibly frustrating that Terence would never do anything to win over his colleagues to his cause. James told his wife Moyra how Terence 'would stalk past his members rather than talk to them'. Moreover, such acts bolstered support for the growing working-class ultra-loyalist movement of Ian Paisley, who was doing everything he could to frustrate O'Neill's reformist agenda. In the previous year Paisley's ceaseless and belligerent rhetoric had already caused the most serious sectarian riots in Belfast for a generation. Terence and Robin came under attack as cowardly traitors for their reforming instincts. Robin received hate mail: he kept one missive, a single sheet of paper sent anonymously through the post, accompanied by a red poppy, bearing the words 'NO SURRENDER'.

Like so many other Unionists, Robin ignored Paisley at first, but as the latter's supporters began infiltrating local con-stituency parties and other Unionist organisations, he soon realised he had to confront him. 'I was', Robin said, 'prob-ably the first Unionist MP to denounce the appalling things Paisley was saying about the minority religion in Northern Ireland.' On 12 July 1966, the day Protestants celebrated the Battle of the Boyne, at a Unionist meeting he was chairing in Belfast, Robin suggested the time had come to counter the threat Paisley represented. It was advice disregarded by others in the Unionist establishment who still didn't take Paisley too seriously. Their failure to do so would eventually destroy the Ulster Unionist party while Robin's criticism of Paisley inside and outside Parliament would be an important factor in bringing his parliamentary career to an end. Robin acknowl-edged that he had got into 'a great deal of trouble' for his attacks on Protestant extremists. Robin was not on his own; his colleagues Stratton Mills and Henry Clark were making the same point. It would cost Clark his Antrim North seat in 1970, which fell to Paisley, who held it until 2010.[5]

Even some of Robin's Unionist colleagues were siding with Paisley over O'Neill's reforms. Knox Cunningham, for example, attacked Robin in an article he wrote for Paisley's newspaper. O'Neill lamented that Cunningham 'regards my policy of decent treatment for all sections of our community as something on the verge of treason'. Yet O'Neill, hindered

---

5 Parliament, RCC; CCLK3/8 Hansard, 4 Nov 1968, cols 517–18

perhaps by his patrician instincts, did little, suggested his rival Brian Faulkner, to build bridges within the party, and his attitude only furthered division within Unionist ranks.[6]

A new generation of more radical nationalist leaders was emerging, influenced by the US civil rights movement which Robin and Jane had witnessed on their visit to the USA. Impatient after years of discrimination, they believed that the pace of change was simply too slow. Political pressure groups were springing up and nationalists took hope from the election of a Labour Government in 1964 when for the first time Unionists could no longer automatically count on the support of the British Government. Harold Wilson, on the other hand, was initially persuaded by O'Neill that reform was taking place as quickly as politically possible. Among nationalists, however, the argument was whether revolution rather than reform was the way to achieve political change.

By 1967, when Terence O'Neill sent a plaintive note to Robin, the situation in Ulster was increasingly tense. 'I would like to say thank-you', he wrote from Stormont in January 1967, 'for all the support and friendship which you showed me in 1966. Everyone from Paisley to Phelim [O'Neill] did everything they could to make it a bloody year and when things were at their worst I always found consolation from talking to you – usually on the telephone!' 'This is a lonely job,' he continued, 'and one seems to be surrounded by critics and enemies. Advice which is both sensible and confidential is not really available here so I fear I shall still contrive to lean on you during 1967.' In the House of Commons there was growing impatience with the speed of reform among influential Labour backbenchers. Gerry Fitt too was increasingly vocal about the need for change. Robin continued to defend O'Neill.

---

6 CCLK1/8 O'Neill to Harold Macmillan, 2 Jun 1967

During a rowdy debate on Northern Ireland in the House of Commons in 1967, replying to Gerry Fitt's condemnation of the lack of progress, Robin insisted that 'improvement has been taking place. It will take place that much faster if it is realised that tensions of generations and scars of history take a long time to heal ... the tensions and difficulties which arise from history are exacerbated by social and economic tensions still apparent in Northern Ireland today.' He was still insisting a year later that there was a chance for men of goodwill on both sides to come together and occupy the middle ground. As he wrote to one correspondent in October 1968, 'Personally, I have fought against fanatics on all sides ever since I have been in politics and that is on record ... there are people, and not all on one side of the political fence, who are striving towards a better future for the whole community.'[7]

It was a difficult fight for Robin. Well aware of the need to press on, he was conscious that he had to tread a fine line if he was to retain the confidence of his local party. 'He wasn't really able to show his moderation as he wanted to,' said his wife Jane. While he was combatting extremism within Unionist ranks, he continued to defend the official Unionist position, which he himself had influenced, as it came under attack from left and right. Yet he relished sparring with opponents in the House. He admitted in later years that personally he actually got on rather well with Gerry Fitt, whom he considered in retrospect a great patriot. In the House of Commons, however, they fought each other no holds barred. Fitt was privately encouraged by Harold Wilson, supported by several Labour backbenchers, to challenge the Unionist status quo in

---

7 CCLK8/1 O'Neill to RCC, 8 Jan 1967; CCLK3/10, Northern Ireland debate, 25 Oct 1967, Hansard, cols 1675–82; CCLK3/28 RCC to D J Brady, 24 Oct 1968

Ulster. Robin, who was still front-bench spokesman for the Conservatives on Northern Ireland, was robust in defence. He did not hesitate to accuse Fitt, in parliamentary terms, of lying, attacking him in one debate as 'the political pedlar of inaccuracies and terminological inexactitudes'. In another, he called him 'as irresponsible a public representative as has ever been elected to this House'.[8]

By now, Catholics were increasingly impatient with O'Neill's failure to turn words into action. The Northern Ireland Civil Rights Association was formed in April 1967 and was soon organising protest marches. Looking back, O'Neill believed that by then the chance to achieve peaceful change had gone. Writing in his memoirs, he observed how

> most of the Unionist Party, not least my predecessor, thought the good old days would just rumble on for ever. A heavy price was to be paid for this attitude. It was not until the start of the Civil Rights movement ... that the more intelligent members of the Party realised that this problem had to be dealt with. By then it was too late.[9]

In the spring of 1968 one consequence of the creeping extremism in Ulster deeply affected Robin. In April his friend Colonel Conolly McCausland died. While he had been a distinguished soldier and a loyal unionist, he was also a Catholic. It was not uncontentious for Protestants, particularly Orangemen, to attend a Catholic requiem mass. There was, moreover, a precedent for this to take place, stretching as far back

8 CCLK3/10, Hansard, 25 Oct 1967, cols 1675–82; CCLK3/8, Hansard, 4 Nov 1968, cols 513–14
9 *The Autobiography of Terence O'Neill, Prime Minister of Northern Ireland 1963–69*, Terence O'Neill, p137

as 1918, when Carson and James Craig attended the requiem mass for John Redmond. But times were changing. In 1962 Ian Paisley had resigned from the Orange Order when it refused to censure the lord mayor of Belfast for his attendance at a Catholic funeral. Although Robin would have gone to the funeral regardless of any advice he was given, he had been told in advance by the Order's Grand Master that his attendance would not breach any of his obligations. Members of his own Orange lodge, the Ballyrashane Loyal Orange Lodge 431, objected. As Robin later recorded, they even held against him that 'I had been educated at "Mag-da-leenie" College, Cambridge, the name being pronounced with venom as to be suggestive of extreme and irrevocable Catholicism.' Robin offered his resignation, which was refused, and he was exonerated from breaking any rules by his local lodge. The objectors, however, were dissatisfied, and the case was taken all the way to the highest body in the Order, the Central Committee of the Grand Lodge of Ireland. This final court imposed on Robin a suspension exactly equal to the time the proceedings had taken since the case was first heard. 'The situation', wrote Robin, 'was risible but the affair had caused distress to a number of people and left a residual threat to my political career.' (One of Robin's close friends, Phelim O'Neill, a Unionist MP at Stormont, was less fortunate, suffering expulsion from the Order in the same year for the same alleged offence.)

On 14 May 1968 the secretary of the Ballyrashane Lodge wrote to Robin, noting how 'in the past you have always been held in high esteem as a Brother Orangeman and staunch Unionist who has done much to uphold the Christian ideals of our Faith'. He hoped that once the facts were known, 'this unhappy incident can be forgotten'. But the letter was written to let Robin know that, with regret, owing to objections from some of his fellow Orangemen, he would not be welcome to sit on the platform for the unveiling ceremony of the lodge's new banner, to the cost of which Robin had made a donation. Loyalist Protestant opinion was hardening.[10]

Catholic opinion was hardening too. If there was to be a place where peaceful protest would spark violence, then a likely contender was the city of Londonderry in Robin's own constituency. The Catholic community there had a long list of grievances, which many had hoped the O'Neill Government would tackle. As one reporter for the *Derry Journal* at the time later noted, 'Derry was overwhelmingly nationalist but gerrymandering, voting restrictions, extra votes for business owners and control of council housing allocation ensured power was held by the leaders of the minority unionist community.'[11]

On Saturday 5 October 1968 members of the Northern Ireland Civil Rights Association defied a ban imposed on their march through Londonderry by an increasingly extreme Bill Craig, now Minister for Home Affairs at Stormont, and were charged by baton-wielding police. It is now seen as the event that triggered what became known as The Troubles, which lasted 30 years, costing the lives of more than 3,700 men, women and children, soldiers and civilians, Protestants and Catholics, injuring more than 47,500 and involving 37,000 shootings and 16,000 bombings. The reason the event captured wider attention than, say, the rioting in Belfast in 1965 was the vivid images captured by photographers and the detailed accounts given by reporters. Gerry Fitt was among the many who were injured, as was Eddie McAteer, the leader of the Nationalist party.

---

10 Personal Papers, S Quinn to RCC, 14 May 1968
11 *Reporting the Troubles: Journalists tell their stories of the Northern Ireland conflict*, compiled by Deric Henderson and Ivan Little, p3

The events in Londonderry sparked further riots and more protests, led the Nationalist party to withdraw from its role as the official opposition at Stormont, hardened opinions within each community and increased the pressure from the Labour Government on O'Neill to accelerate reform. O'Neill, in a letter to Ted Heath, copied to Robin, dated 29 October, emphasised the growth of extremist sentiment among Unionists, who also resented pressure for reform from Westminster and were disdainful of the Labour Government. Any escalation of the situation, he wrote presciently, 'would not only result in the utter ruin of Northern Ireland but incidentally very probably sever the link with Westminster, which at present adds eleven to the voting strength of the Conservative Party'.[12]

While Robin was sympathetic to reform, he was less sympathetic towards the Northern Ireland Civil Rights Association, describing it as an organisation seeking 'to cause dissension and strife in the community, create difficulties for the Government and damage the image of Northern Ireland abroad'. For Unionists, he continued, the Association was 'on a par with any other republican or nationalistic organisation'.[13] This was a view commonly shared by other leading Unionists, such as Brian Faulkner. While Faulkner too acknowledged Catholics had legitimate grievances, the Association, he believed, was no more than a focus for discontent with Unionists and Stormont.

For the first time in living memory the Irish issue took centre stage when the Commons debated the Queen's Speech on 4 November 1968. Harold Wilson had already made clear to Terence O'Neill that events had made the implementation of reform even more urgent and any failure to do so increased

---

12 CCLK3/28
13 CCLK3/28 File on Londonderry Riots, 1967–72

the likelihood of direct intervention by the British Government. During the Commons debate Robin was once again critical of Gerry Fitt, attacking him for his part in leading a parade through a prohibited area. 'For what he has done I cannot forgive him. [He] has undone the work which some of us have been trying to do for years. If I had on my conscience what [he] should have on his, I should find it very hard to live with.' He was responding in the Commons to an equally hard-hitting speech from Fitt, who concluded that, 'if those steps to bring about civil rights, social justice and equal citizenship in Northern Ireland as in other parts of the United Kingdom are not taken, there will be violence and the people will then take to the streets and fight for their rights; and in that fight they will have my whole-hearted support'.[14]

Regardless of his public pronouncements, privately Robin had reached the same conclusion as the British Prime Minister, certainly soon after the events of 5 October and probably sometime before. Robin's brother James was now O'Neill's Minister of Agriculture. Although the brothers were very different, they were very close. Robin was the politician James was not. As Kenneth Bloomfield put it, Robin was 'an articulate and dedicated full-time politician'. 'We were very, very different,' said Robin. 'He was a very straightforward man … he wasn't a politician, he was a person who was a very able soldier.'[15]

Like Terence O'Neill, James looked to Robin for political advice. In the light of the deteriorating situation in Ulster, including worsening relations between the governments at Stormont and Westminster, they both believed Terence was moving much too slowly. Returning to Ross House in

---

14 CCLK3/8, Hansard, 4 Nov 1968, cols 519–20, 510
15 *Stormont in Crisis: A Memoir*, Kenneth Bloomfield, p73; Parliament, RCC

the week of the debate on the Queen's Speech, Robin was mulling over events on the Sunday morning, which happened to be Remembrance Sunday.

> I felt that Northern Ireland's position as part of the UK was, at least in the long term, threatened. In a matter of weeks, particularly since the Civil Rights march of October 5th and rioting in Belfast thereafter, events had seemed to spin out of control. In London a changing attitude towards the ruling party was discernible. Reassuring statements from the Stormont government no longer reassured. It seemed to me things were as bad as I had ever seen them. To give myself hope more than anything else, I reached for a piece of paper and wrote down what seemed to me the essential political and legislative actions which O'Neill and his government should take.[16]

Robin rang Terence to find he was laying a wreath at the war memorial in Londonderry. He then rang James to find his brother had been trying to get in touch with him. Robin decided to drive over to Moyola, piece of paper in his pocket. James told him Bill Craig had contacted him to suggest they should spearhead a drive to remove Terence from office but James had given the idea short shrift. Robin discovered that his brother too had written down a number of recommendations for reform. They combined their ideas into a single paper and rang the hotel where they knew Terence was lunching. He agreed to come over to Moyola, reaching the house in the late afternoon, and listened to what the Chichester-Clark brothers had to say.

'My brother and I', wrote Robin, 'were well aware of the

---

16 Personal Papers, Terence O'Neill's Resignation

almost intractable problems caused by the expectations which O'Neill in his courage, idealism and indeed foresight, had evoked through his utterances and his actions over several years.' They understood how he was being pulled in one direction by diehards in his local party and in another by the British Government.

> Neither of us could have foreseen the depths of his despair that afternoon as he finished reading our submission. Dropping the papers, he declared vehemently, almost indignantly, that he could see no glimmer of hope that he could get anything like our proposals through his Unionist party, and within a few minutes he had gone. It was, I think, from that moment that my brother's limited faith in his leader drained away.[17]

On reflection, however, Terence decided to make one last push for change. Finally, on 22 November, after numerous Cabinet meetings where the arguments went back and forth, the Stormont Government was able to announce a programme of action which bore a strong resemblance to the plans sketched out by the Chichester-Clark brothers. At the same time, Robin arranged lunch in a pub opposite Parliament for those Unionist MPs at Westminster who were sympathetic to reform to persuade them to support O'Neill's programme. The proposals included the abolition of Londonderry's corporation and its replacement by the Londonderry Development Corporation as well as measures to reform the system of housing allocations and the local government franchise. For a brief period Terence O'Neill enjoyed an upsurge in popular support and his party gave him a vote of confidence. But it was too little, too late, and the plans further

---

17 Personal Papers, Terence O'Neill's Resignation

divided the Unionist party. Several resignations took place, including Brian Faulkner's, and there was mounting pressure on Terence to resign. After a series of further protests and an escalation in violence during January 1969, he was prompted to call a General Election, which proved a disastrous move. Unionist party candidates split into two groups, Official Unionists and Unofficial Unionists. The Unionist majority was reduced, there was an upsurge in support for Paisley and his followers and in his own constituency Terence O'Neill only just held off Paisley himself.

Although O'Neill pushed through his package of reforms in the ensuing months, this did nothing to quell the violence. On Saturday 19 April there was serious rioting in the Bogside area of Londonderry as clashes once again occurred between the Civil Rights Association and the police. One man, who had taken no part in the demonstration, was severely beaten by police after they entered his house, and died soon afterwards as a result. On the next day Robin as the constituency MP visited the area. The following Tuesday, as a result of the violence, a debate on Northern Ireland took place in the Commons. Robin took part but had the misfortune to speak immediately before the 21-year-old Bernadette Devlin, who was making her maiden speech after winning the by-election for Mid-Ulster. (She had previously stood without success against James Chichester-Clark in the elections for Stormont in February.) Robin had repeated his previous condemnation of the civil rights movement, describing it as an out-of-control monster captured by extremists. In her response, Bernadette Devlin took aim at Robin, attacking him as an establishment Unionist out of touch with the views of the working class and as a representative of 'a bigoted and sectarian Unionist party'. Lambasting the O'Neill Government for its inadequate reform programme, her words encapsulated the enduring discrimination suffered by the Catholic community in Ulster. In its anger, the speech symbolised the ever-widening gulf between the two communities and the narrowing space left in Northern Ireland for politicians like Robin with moderate views.

By then, Robin knew that the O'Neill Government was about to fall. The catalyst would be the resignation of his brother James from the O'Neill Cabinet. The pretext would be a pledge James had given to his constituency party that he would not for the time being vote in favour of any change to the local government franchise, although this was something he favoured in principle. In reality, as Robin recalled, James believed Terence 'could no longer summon up the confidence and support of his party to take it any further along the path of change'. It was a move the brothers hoped would hasten the end of his time in office.[18]

In his memoirs, O'Neill suggests that James's ultimate decision to resign was made almost on the spur of the moment, whereas in fact it had clearly been in his mind for some time. O'Neill had already stated that he would resign if he failed to win local government reform. Kenneth Bloomfield phoned Robin to ask him to persuade his brother not to resign but Robin declined. James resigned on 23 April 1968. He received his fair share of criticism. As his wife Moyra recalled, 'everyone thought James was behaving as badly as Faulkner but he resigned in good faith'. O'Neill recorded how one of his colleagues told James that what he had done might lead to Ulster's downfall. O'Neill's daughter told reporters her father had been stabbed in the back. Faulkner and his supporters believed it was all part of a plot to raise James's profile as O'Neill's chosen successor in advance of O'Neill's resignation,

18 Personal Papers, Terence O'Neill's Resignation

all done, wrote Faulkner, 'to ensure that power was kept in the hands of the "Big House"'. When James called on O'Neill the morning after his resignation, O'Neill, still convinced that James's decision had been almost unintentional, felt that James 'was genuinely upset that he had set all this in motion'. When Robin returned home at the end of the week, he

> took a painful call from O'Neill [who said] that as a result of my brother's defection he had felt unable to continue in office. He suggested that he should call and see me on his way to Stormont. His visit was one that I shall not forget. Jane ... brought a cup of coffee to a grim-faced O'Neill in the drawing room. Memorably, she greeted him with the comment, 'I want you to know that I think my brother-in-law has behaved most irresponsibly.' It was a point of view but I did not share it. Terence expressed his dismay that I should appear to desert him at last. Some remarks, probably unworthy of both [of us] were made, and he was on his way. It was virtually the end of a long friendship and ... we spoke again but rarely.

The depth of the chasm that opened up between the two former friends is evident from O'Neill's memoirs, in which there is not a single mention of Robin. Yet O'Neill came to express regret that change had not come more quickly, writing to Robin on 21 October 1969, 'If only we could have had reform sooner, we wouldn't have had revolution now, along with semi-direct rule from London.'[19]

Robin persuaded his brother he had to stand for the

---

19 *Memoirs of a Statesman*, Brian Faulkner, p54; *The Autobiography of Terence O'Neill, Prime Minister of Northern Ireland 1963–1969*, pp125–29; Parliament, RCC; Personal Papers, Terence O'Neill to RCC 21 Oct 1969

leadership of the party and thus the premiership. Although James was a reluctant candidate, he had a strong sense of duty; as Kenneth Bloomfield observed, 'James never ached to become Prime Minister. He was a good soldier doing his duty.' On the day before Stormont MPs voted for a new leader, Robin wrote, 'Poor James, I wouldn't wish what may be coming to him upon him but someone has got to do this ghastly job and thank God it can't be and isn't me. I rather think that he will get it and [I] feel ashamed that I spent most of last weekend twisting both his and Moyra's arms into having a shot at it.' The election took place on 1 May: James won by a single vote over his rival Brian Faulkner. That vote came from his predecessor, Terence O'Neill. 'It seemed odd,' wrote O'Neill, 'that I should vote for the man who had brought me down, but it had been due to the worries and doubts in his very unpolitical mind ... in any event, I couldn't bring myself to vote for the man [Faulkner] who had been trying to bring me down for six years.' After James returned to Moyola on the day of his election, his daughter Tara remembered hearing the sound of music coming from the bottom of the avenue leading up to the house: it was the band of the local Orange lodge, celebrating the success of one of their own.[20]

20 CCLK3/17 Papers on Bernadette Devlin etc, RCC to Patricia Stephenson-Clark, 30 Apr 1969; *The Autobiography of Terence O'Neill*, p129

Chapter Five

OVERTAKEN BY EVENTS

As Prime Minister, James Chichester-Clark did indeed have 'a ghastly job'. All the tensions that had been building up under Terence O'Neill came to a head almost as soon as he had taken up office. There was a forlorn feeling to Robin's statement to the press when his brother became Prime Minister: 'He is tough, he is straight and he will do what he believes to be right. One now hopes that everyone will rally round. It is a terribly tough job and I am praying for him.' This was reflected in much of the press comment too, with many commentators predicting James's tenure would be short-lived. One of them spelt out the conundrum facing him: he had to win over the right of his own party and those who supported Paisley while trying to push through reforms acceptable to civil rights supporters whose enthusiasm for the changes on offer was waning rapidly. It seemed an impossible challenge yet James did succeed in completing O'Neill's reform programme. He brought Brian Faulkner back into the Cabinet, who later wrote how he found James to be 'a loyal and helpful colleague with whom to work; he was honest and direct and I gained a new respect for him'. He was, said Faulkner, 'a big man with a big heart'.[1]

Simply completing what had already been started, however, would no longer be enough. The list of demands from the civil rights movement grew longer. Protests continued and

---

1 *Memoirs of a Statesman*, Brian Faulkner, p56, p67

violence increased. Robin was anxious to spend as much time as he could in Ulster to support his brother. He was critical of the pressure the Labour Government was putting on his brother to speed up the reform process even further. Ironically, given his criticism of Terence O'Neill, Robin believed accelerating change without winning the support of the majority community could only result, as he later said, in the people of Ulster paying the price 'in blood, houses and jobs'. Their sister Penelope wondered 'whether James's career as Prime Minister and all that would have happened if Robin hadn't propped him up. He prepared James and advised James and was enormously committed to him in that way.' But the fact was that the middle ground occupied by the brothers' moderate brand of Unionism was shrinking rapidly.[2]

Robin found himself under attack from both sides as he stuck valiantly to his beliefs and continued to speak out against extremism wherever it was found. He was weighed down by the pressures of representing a constituency riven by sectarian strife, tied to a Conservative party with a diminishing interest in sustaining the Unionists, criticised as a member of the Unionist establishment against whose influence Paisley was in part building up his support, a moderate reformer supporting a programme seen as too little, too late, whose views were being eliminated from the system by extremists on both sides. He was, said his daughter Emma, 'pretty stressed out most of the time'. The crisis in his constituency demanded his full attention at weekends back from Westminster, which, combined with the travelling back and forth every week, and a limited salary gobbled up by parliamentary expenses, placed him under increasing strain, especially as the tide of events turned against him.

---

2 Hansard, Home Affairs, 3 Jul 1970, col 242

The family felt the impact of all this. Robin often had to curtail his time with them when they were on holiday – 'we longed for him not to go,' recalled Emma – and sometimes he was unable to be with them at all. A popular destination each summer was the west coast of Donegal. The family would take two cars, each laden with children, dogs and luggage. Robin's son Mark remembered how competitive his father and mother could be, racing each other along narrow country lanes, his father not averse to giving Jane's car a gentle nudge.

Often the family were joined by Diana Young, a university friend of Jane's, and her four children, and more occasionally by Murray and Joan Stuart-Smith and their six children. Murray, later a distinguished Appeal Court judge, had known Jane at Cambridge and subsequently became friends with Robin as well. Murray's wife Joan, it turned out, was a distant relation of Terence O'Neill. They stayed once on Teelin Pier under dramatic Slieve League, more usually in the village of Malin Beg, close to the beautiful horseshoe-shaped Silver Strand beach. 'We adored going there,' said Mark. 'It was a lovely place.' Murray would build incredible dams, there were sandcastles, climbing and some walking. (One of Murray's sandcastles, recalled Mark, was so fantastic, it was photographed for *National Geographic*.) Murray would bring a Shakespeare play with him, and everyone would take a part, acting it out on top of the cliffs overlooking the sea. In a superficial attempt to mask his identity in a republican part of the country, Robin called himself Mr Clark, but this did not prevent him from being identified. He was often threatening to cancel holidays for fear of threats to the family over the border. Eventually, such threats were made, bringing these holidays to an end. 'We were there [Malin Beg] in August 1969,' said Mark, when things were coming to a height in Derry with him ringing and telling us all to come back. I suspect it was the day before the announcement that troops were to be sent in from England. There was only one phone in the village, in the post office, and someone came rushing down the street to the cottage, saying we were needed on the phone. I remember following my mother to the post office. The phone was in a cubicle, and the post mistress would frantically wind a handle on another phone and then summon one into the cubicle. I stood outside when my mother went in. She came out ashen faced. It was my father saying that we had to come home that night. He didn't feel it was safe for us to be there. It was very dramatic. We packed everything up and left.

At Ross House the ground-floor windows were bomb-proofed; with regular death threats, security personnel were stationed in the boiler house in the yard and Robin kept a shotgun at the bottom of the bed. Although the family dogs were no real threat, one timid, the other deaf, they did see off one set of intruders. Anonymous phone calls were frequently made to the house. 'There was a speaker system for the front door,' remembered Mark, 'which my father had no idea how to operate, because he wasn't technically minded at all.' Similarly, although Robin was advised to check under his car for bombs, he did so for years without ever really understanding what he was looking for. 'We were told to be very vigilant about any parcels that were suspicious,' said Mark.

One day in the spring of 1974 we received one such parcel with the address written in capital letters and a questionable post-mark. We carried it gingerly some distance from the house and called the security services. Before long there was a tremendous noise overhead as the army arrived by helicopter and landed in the field. When the parcel turned out to be some linen table napkins sent as a wedding present by a constituent we all felt embarrassed particularly when I discovered that the helicopter consumed 32 gallons of petrol an hour.

It was stressful, Robin recalled, but he became phlegmatic about it: 'If the sun comes out the next day, you suddenly forget about it.' This was not the whole story: Robin rarely spoke to friends and colleagues about the stresses and strains of being an Ulster MP. His friend, the Labour MP Ray Carter, recalled that 'these things were so deeply personal to him that we never discussed them'. Keeping so much to himself probably contributed to the severe depression Robin suffered several years after leaving politics altogether. It was only many years later that Robin was reassured that he was no longer a target in Ulster. By then he was working in London, and his colleague Alistair Colgrain remembered Robin arriving in the office the day after he had received the news: 'He looked incredibly peaceful.'[3]

Threats were also made to kidnap the children when they were at boarding school on the mainland. The children were unaware that for a while they were placed under surveillance. Emma was at school in Kent, flying from Belfast with her pet white rabbit, Dandelion, in a basket on her knee, along with a small suitcase and huge trunk. Her father would collect her from the terminal building in Cromwell Road in London and take her to catch the train from Victoria station. She once ran away from school because she wasn't very happy. This got her into a lot of trouble and made her parents equally angry.

---

3 Parliament, RCC

She worried that nobody would collect her for her next exeat, but when she arrived at Victoria she was relieved to find her father waiting for her, stern but understanding. It was only in her mid-teens that Emma began to sense the tension in Ulster. Invitations to parties at distant destinations were accompanied by doubts over whether or not the journey would be safe to take. With the security measures in place at home, 'we almost felt like hostages,' she said. 'I was quite scared sometimes because we felt quite vulnerable where we were at the end of this long, long drive, and I did have dreams about the IRA marching down the drive in the middle of the night.'

Mark followed St George's, Windsor, with a place at Eton. His father wrote to him regularly, sometimes took him out for the afternoon and occasionally brought him into the House of Commons. 'He was very good at keeping my spirits up because he knew how much I hated going back at the end of the day.' When Mark called home from school, reversing the charges, Robin would pull the operator's leg, pretending he had no idea who might be calling him. On Mark's first day at Eton, after having said his goodbyes, Robin suddenly reappeared at the door of Mark's room, having turned his car around on reaching the M4, worried that his son might not know how to tie his tie.

Politics clouded Robin's marriage. Jane was increasingly unsympathetic towards the Unionist cause, which, she admitted, 'was not helpful'. 'I tried to understand and I tried to assimilate myself to it but as it went on through the years, I found the more I knew, the less I liked it; and I'm afraid to say it was politics as much as anything else that caused the disruption of our marriage.' She became a supporter of the nationalist politician John Hume, who would help to found the Social and Democratic Labour Party with Gerry Fitt and others in 1970. 'James and Robin', she said, 'didn't trust him

and for me that was a great barrier because I couldn't understand it and more and more of my sympathy was going the
wrong way.'

In the months following James Chichester-Clark becoming
Prime Minister, there were more riots. At the beginning of
August 1969, James discussed increasing the number of security personnel in the province with the Home Secretary, James
Callaghan. They also agreed that the annual Apprentice Boys
march could take place in Londonderry. At the time, despite
the protests and the violence, there still seemed hope for the
moderate path planned by the Chichester-Clark brothers. An
editorial in *The Guardian* prior to the parade noted that civil
rights activism and liberal Unionism were achieving reform,
but warned that too many civil rights supporters were raising
the issue of partition, which served only to harden the views
of those on the other side of the argument.

On the day of the parade, Sunday 12 August, Robin had
invited a small group of Westminster MPs to join him as
observers. As well as his Unionist colleagues Stratton Mills,
Rafton Pounder and Jack Maginnis, the group included Conservative MP Nigel Fisher. After attending the service in the
cathedral, they spent the day watching the parade, leaving it
after the procession reached Waterloo Square. They returned
to the square when they heard rioting had broken out. They
found the two sides confronting each other with police in
helmets and riot shields between them. 'I walked among the
Protestant crowd,' wrote Robin shortly afterwards, 'asking
them to disperse and leave the matter in the hands of the
police. The vast majority of those present were taking a
reasonable attitude although there were a few from places
other than Londonderry upon whom any such appeal was
lost.' The situation steadily deteriorated, the first petrol bomb
was thrown, Robin borrowed a loudhailer and asked the

Protestant crowd to go home. 'I made three appeals which had some effect on all but a very small group.' During the evening he witnessed the rioting in William Street, Waterloo Street and Sackville Street. He agreed with the police that the use of tear gas had become 'inevitable'. The police, he believed, behaved 'immaculately'. He finally left London-derry at two in the morning. He returned later that day to help find accommodation for residents who had been threat-ened with being burnt out, then left for Belfast to report to the Stormont Government. On 14 August he flew to London to meet Opposition leaders, returning to Londonderry the next day to deal with those needing shelter.[4]

After two days of continuous rioting, the police were clearly overstretched. James Chichester-Clark asked for military assis-tance. The British Government insisted Stormont should use all the resources at its disposal before this happened, stressing that such a move would fundamentally alter the relationship between the two governments. The part-time 'B' Specials were called up but they were simply not equipped to deal with the violence. On the same day that Robin had flown to London, troops were deployed for the first time on the streets of Ulster, entering Londonderry that afternoon. A few days later both governments issued a joint communiqué stressing that the constitutional arrangement between the two sides had not changed, which was clearly not the case. This was evident from James's decision to place responsibility for secu-rity in the province in the hands of the general commanding the troops rather than an elected representative. Whether or not James had discussed this with Robin, it highlighted the fact that James was more soldier than politician.

In the aftermath of the rioting, Robin made every effort

---

4 CCLK3/27, RCC's written recollections of the events of 12 August 1969

to help his colleagues in the Commons understand what was going on in Ulster. He hosted several groups of Conservative MPs on fact-finding visits which Robin believed helped to dispel myths. He also wanted people to discover, as one of his colleagues put it, 'the wealth of moderate Protestant opinion'. He was, as always, the most welcoming of hosts. As another MP, David Renton, wrote to him on 4 September 1969, 'The pleasure of meeting your enchanting family, staying in the house which you have both made so lovely, guzzling the delicious meals you provided, enjoyable and informative conversation, while being driven at reasonable speeds in your car – all of these together made "fact finding" easy and less unpleasant than it could have been.'[5]

At the same time, however, there was growing opposition among Unionists to the path Ulster was taking under James Chichester-Clark. There was resentment at the threat to Ulster's devolved government from the changing relationship between Stormont and Westminster. There was unhappiness at the decision to give a British army officer control of Ulster's security, compounded by the disbandment of the 'B' Specials in favour of creating the Ulster Defence Regiment, with James coming under attack for dismantling what was seen, in Kenneth Bloomfield's words, as 'a bulwark of the unionist state'. Moreover, as Robin recalled, James was also under fire for continuing to press for reform while the bombs were going off and his constituency association was losing confidence in him. There was an ugly incident as James emerged from a meeting of his constituency association in Maghera in August 1970 when he was faced with a jeering mob of Paisley supporters. His wife Moyra recalled how local

5 CCLK3/27, Northern Ireland, Aug–Oct 1969, Peter Kirk, MP, quoted in *The Irish Times*, 3 Sep 1969; David Renton to RCC, 4 Sep 1969

hardliners marched up the avenue to Moyola carrying an empty coffin although James was away at the time. Members of James's own Cabinet were wavering in their support. Nevertheless, Robin reflected, James 'actually got through more reforms than any of the other prime ministers and in much greater difficulty because he couldn't control security'.[6]

By then, a new government had taken office in London. In June 1970 Harold Wilson's Labour party was surprisingly beaten at the polls by Ted Heath's Conservatives. With the support of the eight Ulster Unionist MPs, Heath achieved a majority of 31 seats. Everyone expected Robin to be given a ministerial position. The whips had suggested he might become Minister for the Arts or Minister of State at the Board of Trade. After waiting for some time at Ross House on the day after the election, Robin was contacted by Downing Street, asking him to travel to Belfast to await a call on the secure line from the new Prime Minister. Ted had disappointing news for Robin: it was politically unwise, he told Robin, for the brother of the Northern Ireland Prime Minister to hold ministerial office in a Conservative Government since future events in such turbulent times might cause an embarrassing resignation. The let-down – which it was, coming from a long-standing friend – was, Robin recalled later with some understatement, 'disappointing', but he agreed with Ted, who said they should keep in touch. He asked Robin to continue to advise him on Northern Ireland and promised he would come back to him with an offer of a post as soon as was politically expedient. Here, however, was another sign that the traditional ties between the Unionist and Conservative parties were weakening. In public, however, Robin insisted he had no wish to serve in the Government, preferring the freedom to comment on Ulster affairs.

---

6 *A Tragedy of Errors*, Kenneth Bloomfield, p20; Parliament, RCC

In returning just eight Unionist MPs, Northern Ireland's 1970 election results highlighted the fracturing of support for the Unionists, who had lost two more seats compared with the 1966 election. Henry Clark lost to Ian Paisley in Antrim North and James Hamilton lost to the nationalist and civil rights activist Frank McManus in Fermanagh and South Tyrone. On 19 May 1970 *The Irish Times* reported that Paisley's Protestant Unionists saw Robin as 'particularly unsatisfactory', but were reluctant to put up a candidate for fear of splitting the Unionist vote. In fact, allegations surfaced during the campaign that Robin had reached an accommodation with Paisley's supporters to prevent this happening, allegations he vigorously rebutted. He won support from Ted Heath, who copied to Robin a note he had sent on 12 June 1970, a week before election day, to John Hume, in which he stressed that Robin had 'made no bargains with anybody'. In a letter sent to *The Times* on 26 June 1970 Robin set out how he had attacked Paisley and his policies during the election, referring to 'my determination to fight sectarian politics and intolerance wherever I find it'. He had discovered just after the election that Paisley supporters had infiltrated his constituency association. A week later, speaking in the home affairs debate in the Commons, Robin was unhesitatingly critical of Paisley, who had already spoken. 'I cannot see in his political behaviour', said Robin,

the love, charity and forgiveness which I expect of Protestantism, whether it be in politics or anywhere else … Perhaps to some extent all of us in Northern Ireland share the guilt that we have allowed this inflated bubble to expand to its present size without having pricked it long ago. There have been fence sitters and far too many who have held back for fear of offending one section or another. For my part, I want it known in this House and further afield that I will fight this man and what he stands for as long as I can and as hard as I have fought anyone who has damaged the good name of the British people in Northern Ireland or elsewhere ... No doubt, there will be further smears and more intimidation, but I really do not care. I am one of those who have tried time and time again to explain to those in Northern Ireland just what would be at risk if they followed, through fear, a course which is alien to the whole British tradition of fairness and justice. I have told them that by doing that they will put at risk their constitution and their place in the United Kingdom which I have passionately defended for a long time in this House.

Until the end of his life Robin was convinced Paisley's actions led to loss of life in Northern Ireland. 'I challenged him time and time again in the House of Commons. He made me ashamed to come from the same part of the world as he did.' As Robin wrote later, the unfounded allegation that he would ally himself with Paisley 'hurt my feelings and has rankled with me over the years like no other assertion made against me in my political career. No doubt it is some sort of vanity that it still gives me distress that a limited number of people may have believed that I would abandon my own conviction as to right and wrong in so deplorable a way.'[7]

In his speech Robin had criticised the actions of the Apprentice Boys, whose general secretary wrote him a stinging rebuke, but one which again clearly showed which way politics was moving in Ulster. Attacking Robin for his

---

7 Personal Papers, Ted Heath to John Hume, 12 Jun 1970; CCLK1/10
RCC to *The Times*, 26 Jun 1970; Hansard, Home Affairs, 3 Jul 1970, col 248;
Parliament, RCC; Personal Papers, notes on the 'Paisley Smear'

'unjustifiable outburst', James Guy went on to defend Paisley. 'His courage and forthrightness have been a bulwark to many in these troubled times,' he wrote. Recent events, he contin- ued, have 'vindicated utterly the truth and force of many of his pronouncements'. 'You appear to be guilty of the very bigotry and intolerance you decry in others,' Guy concluded. 'We can have no further confidence in you as our representa- tive so long as you maintain the attitudes displayed in your remarks of yesterday.' In his reply, Robin pointed out how he had made clear where he stood on Paisley at several meet- ings during the election, one of which Guy had attended. His speech, he said, had been intended to restore the credibility of Ulster which Paisley had done so much to damage. He noted that no one from the Apprentice Boys had come to his defence when he had been called a liar by Paisley. 'I intend to go on defending the Constitution', he wrote, 'against anyone who in my opinion endangers it.'[8]

On the same day James Guy was writing his letter, Robin was appearing alongside Gerry Fitt on Radio 4's *The Week In Westminster*. In public, he tried hard to play down Paisley's importance, a line shared by Fitt, stating that he was 'per- fectly confident that next time [Paisley] will be put out [of his constituency]. He is not a threat to the Unionist Party in Northern Ireland at all.' It is difficult to believe Robin said this with any sincerity. The two men had different interpretations of recent events. Fitt believed reform would never have taken place in Ulster without a Labour Government, Robin stated the process was already underway; Fitt considered the Orange parades were provocative and insulting, Robin praised the

---

8 CCLK1/10, James Guy, General Secretary, General Committee, Apprentice Boys of Derry, to RCC, 4 Jul 1970, and RCC to James Guy, 13 Jul 1970

Order for its statesmanlike approach in voluntarily stopping some parades and re-routing others. A week later Robin was taking to task Dr Hillery, Éire's Minister for External Affairs, for asking the Orange Order to cancel their annual parades as a contribution towards reducing fear and tension in the province. This, said Robin, was asking the Order 'to abandon the civil right upon which they place the greatest value at the present time and the one which they have enjoyed, almost invariably peacefully, for generations'. Hillery replied that he had in fact only asked for the parades to be re-routed rather than cancelled.

Released from front-bench responsibilities, Robin was taking advantage of his freedom to comment on matters in Northern Ireland. As he had shown in his response to Dr Hillery, he was at the forefront of pressing the official Unionist line. Although he had done this throughout his political life, he clearly felt it was now more important than ever. Just as he never shirked from attacking Ian Paisley, he never turned down an invitation to debate with Bernadette Devlin. At the end of December 1970, he sat alongside both of them for an Ulster TV programme, although appearing on television was never something he enjoyed. Robin's son accompanied him to the studios in Belfast where he introduced Mark to Paisley and Devlin. 'Even though I knew he didn't have much time for them, he still exchanged friendly banter with them before and after, although it was a very heated interview.' It was one of Robin's characteristics that however much he might disagree with an opponent, he always treated them as fellow human beings. Robin came under fire from Paisley and Devlin for, despite their opposing views, they both shared the belief that much of Ulster's troubles could be attributed to the Anglo-Irish landed establishment's monopoly of power. Unlike his attitude to Paisley, Robin was never quite sure how to respond to Bernadette Devlin, constrained somewhat by his natural courtesy.[9]

In the House of Commons, Robin helped to loosen further the ties of loyalty between Unionists and Conservatives, leading his colleagues in a targeted campaign of voting against the Government as a way of protesting at its handling of Northern Ireland, now the responsibility of the new Home Secretary, Reginald Maudling, although they were careful not to cause undue embarrassment. Robin had written to the Chief Whip, Francis Pym, in November 1970, telling him how he and his colleagues disapproved of the Government's current policy of 'benevolent neutrality' and as a result felt under no obligation to support the Government, although they would strive to do so on key issues. Privately, Robin felt disappointed in Ted Heath, who he believed never really got to grips with the situation, despite all the advice Robin offered him. Robin also compared Maudling unfavourably to his predecessor, James Callaghan, who had earned widespread respect for his handling of matters in Northern Ireland. Maudling's career would eventually end in disgrace as a result of his involvement in the Poulson corruption scandal. Robin had already seen the character weaknesses that would contribute to Maudling's downfall. There was the empty brandy bottle left beneath his bed after he and his wife had stayed with Robin's brother James at Moyola. (Drinks offered at Moyola were never less than very generous.) More importantly, there was also, Robin wrote later,

---

9 Years later, after Robin and Jane had separated, Jane saw Ian Paisley at Belfast Airport. They were both standing in queues for the check-in. Paisley recognised her and gave her an ingratiating smile. Jane never forgot what he had done to Robin, and, furrowing her brow, she mouthed very obviously, allowing for no misinterpretation, 'You bastard'

an innate laziness, together with a certain lack of emotional imagination, [which] made it hard for him to understand the fears, feelings and compulsions of generations raised on decades of inadequate and atavistic renderings of history ... Nor was he more successful in grasping the restraints imposed upon those moderates who could sometimes see through the tangle of their own loyalties and emotions and who struggled ... to show the way for others.[10]

Outside Parliament, Robin took speaking engagements to try to give people an idea of what it felt like to be a Unionist in Ulster. Speaking to the Leeds University Conservative Association in January 1971, he told his audience how 'two cultures – two heritages – side by side [were] a classical recipe for strife. Both sides jealously cultivate their separate identities. A considerable proportion of the Roman Catholic minority gives its prime allegiance to an alien government in Dublin and at best acquiesces to the Acts of the Stormont Government. A smaller number ... condone and even actively advocate violent methods of subversion.' There was no viable opposition in Ulster, he continued, where the vast majority of people would be unwilling to accept anything other than a Unionist government.[11]

Robin was struggling against the prevailing winds. The situation in Northern Ireland was steadily worsening. In January 1971 the Ulster Unionist Council called for James Chichester-Clark to resign. On Saturday 6 February 1971 the IRA murdered Gunner Robert Curtis, the first British soldier to die in

---

10 CCLK3/11, RCC to Francis Pym, 6 Nov 1970; Personal Papers, Notes on Maudling and Heath, Mar 2007
11 CCLK3/22, Speech to Leeds University Conservative Association, 15 Jan 1971

the conflict. When three more soldiers were killed in March while they were off-duty in Belfast, James found himself under almost unbearable pressure. He travelled to London where he believed he had extracted a promise of more troops only for the promise to be broken by Lord Carrington as Secretary of State for Defence when he visited Belfast a few days later. When Robin subsequently heard Al Haig as US Secretary of State call Carrington 'a duplicitous bastard' during the Falklands crisis, it was, he said, the best description of Carrington he had ever heard.

James had had enough. He resigned on 20 March 1971. In spite of the pressure he was under, his decision still came as a surprise. Even his wife Moyra didn't know he was going to resign. 'I was shopping in Belfast and I happened to pass a television shop and there was James on the television.' Initially, recalled Robin's wife Jane, both Moyra and Robin were upset with James's action: 'they believed he was letting everyone down'. They soon revised their views and Robin strongly defended his brother in public, regretting that James's achievement in pushing through change had been so little recognised by the nationalist community.

For the Conservative party conference in Brighton the following October, Robin prepared a speech which in part paid tribute to his brother. He never got to deliver it and he felt he was deliberately denied the opportunity to speak. The surviving draft shows Robin's despair, even bitterness, at the turn of events in Northern Ireland. As one of those, he said, who had outlined 'early tentative steps which might break down the centuries old wall of suspicion and mistrust, I see our dream lying in tatters'. He lamented the fact that 'Northern Ireland, we are told, is now down to its last moderate leader,' something he still refused to accept. He took a tough line on military intervention, pressing his brother's case that 'specific and swift action' was needed to take on the IRA before the violence worsened. The army, wrote Robin, should 'get on with the job without one hand tied behind its back'. He criticised once again the failure of mainland opinion to recognise the seriousness of the situation: 'Many good, solid, decent citizens in Ulster are aghast and uncomprehending that the peoples of Britain beside whom they stood in war and peace seem hesitant to give them their wholehearted backing in their hour of need.'

James was succeeded by Brian Faulkner, who was sympathetic to his predecessor: 'He left a job in which he had done his duty as an officer and a gentleman but which I doubt if he ever really wanted.'[12] Robin was never close to Brian Faulkner. Like others, he regarded Faulkner as untrustworthy, a plotter and follower of bandwagons. Nevertheless, he did his best to keep him apprised of the British Government's latest views on Northern Ireland, although Faulkner did not always listen. Faulkner would spend even less time in office than James Chichester-Clark. Although his decision to reintroduce internment (arrest and detention without trial) in August 1971 had the backing of the British Government, he was told that its failure would precipitate the end of Stormont. Internment only increased tension in the province, giving protestors another grievance and setting off another round of marches. Both James and Robin opposed internment. James said immediately that it would be a disaster while Robin believed it would never work unless it was introduced on both sides of the border. Both James and Robin felt it would sweep up too many innocent men who would then be seen as martyrs. On the other hand, Robin attacked the lack of any alternative offered by nationalist leaders.

---

12 *Memoirs of a Statesman*, Brian Faulkner, p75

It was not a happy time in Robin's life. The pressures were immense and, looking back, he admitted to feeling under 'emotional strain'. To the distress of his children, his marriage to Jane was falling apart, and much to her later regret, she left Robin during 1971. 'It just seemed inevitable that we could not go on,' recalled Jane. Politics, money and absence from home all played their part. Jane had met Paddy Falloon, whose daughter was a friend of Robin and Jane's daughter Emma. He was completely different from Robin, an older, self-made man, who shared common interests with Jane in a relationship that lacked the competitive edge evident between her and Robin. The separation and divorce, which came through at the beginning of 1972, 'was all pretty awful', said Mark Chichester-Clark. Immediately before the divorce proceedings, Mark rang his father from Eton, pleading with him not to go through with it. For the family it was not only a very divisive time emotionally, with loyalties being stretched, it was also physically divisive, since the law in Northern Ireland required a divorcing couple to sleep in separate houses within a certain time period of the proceedings. Until the divorce came through, the couple lived separately, Jane returning to Ross House with their daughters, Robin taking Mark to live with him at Moyola.

Robin could never forgive Paddy Falloon for breaking up the marriage, even though he was always perfectly charming in Paddy's company whenever they met in future years. And ultimately Robin and Jane would repair their relationship: they would call each other from time to time and each attended the other's 80th birthday party as well as other family events. 'I miss those telephone calls,' reflected Jane. 'I did grow to appreciate what a really lovely man he was, and I regret that what we had to go through was so destructive. But it wasn't set up to make a good marriage, having this Irish Sea between us.'

Re-establishing that relationship, however, took many years. Things were desperately difficult at the time of the separation as Emma and Fia took their mother's side, Mark his father's. 'It had an enormous effect on us all,' said Mark. 'I have many memories of [my father's] anger and hurt, and on one occasion, hidden tears at Moyola when we were sleeping there, but more obviously his need to talk about it whenever we met.' It weakened the strength of the bond between Emma and her father, which recovered only in the early 1980s when they rebuilt their earlier close relationship over regular lunches together. Although Emma began to confide in her father once again, 'I don't think he ever forgot.' Fia too, just nine years old, found it took her several years to get to know her father again.[13]

Emma knew her father was devastated on the day her mother left and that he felt his world was collapsing around him. Even so, there was light as well as dark, thanks to Robin's sense of humour; 'We always had a very good time, with plenty of good humour,' Mark recalled. He remembered the kindness of the Stoney family, their close friends in County Antrim, Thomas Stoney being rector of Broughshane. Robin worked hard to keep the family together after Jane left. 'He did everything he could to keep it all going,' said Emma. 'He was determined to protect us and look after us.' Robin employed girls from Australia and New Zealand to help run the household during the holidays. His mother Marion and sister Penelope stepped in to help out. The study became a breakfast room, a new bedroom was made for Emma at the top of the house, Fia moved into Emma's old bedroom and accommodation was created for a couple to live in and look after the property when no one else was there. Robin

---

13 Parliament, RCC

even made a drawing table for Emma which she still uses. For Fia, however, the youngest of the children, much of whose childhood seems in retrospect to have been dominated by her parents' deteriorating marriage, the changes made to Ross House seemed to define the end of one era and the start of another. Sent away to boarding school, she returned home to find Ross House completely changed.

Politically, 1972 was also a terrible year for Robin. The tragedy of Bloody Sunday took place in his constituency on 30 January. Robin was devastated by the killings of 13 men, all of them Catholics. He had been so anxious about the impending march that on the Saturday night he had visited Londonderry to speak to Brigadier Pat MacLellan, commanding British troops in the city, who assured him that the army was well prepared. Instead, the local commander ignored the orders for a limited intervention, sending in his men in force, creating the running battle that ended in so many deaths at the hands of British troops. Robin, said his friend and fellow MP Stratton Mills, knew this spelled the end of the Stormont Government. (In 2010, when Lord Saville published his report into Bloody Sunday, Robin welcomed its conclusions, which confirmed what he had always believed. Writing to David Cameron in July 2010, he noted how in the immediate aftermath of the event, 'reports much at variance with what I had been led to believe began to gain credibility'. Bloody Sunday, he continued, was 'a happening of which every decent British person must feel a mixture of shame and revulsion'.) As Kenneth Bloomfield wrote, 'internment followed by Bloody Sunday radicalised large elements of the nationalist community and persuaded all too many of their young men in particular that democratic means alone would never adequately protect their rights and interests'. Less than a month later, the first bomb planted by the IRA on the mainland went off at

Aldershot barracks, killing seven people, including a Catholic padre. In Northern Ireland, bomb attacks and shootings became more frequent and more murderous.[14]

An emergency debate on Northern Ireland took place in the Commons on 1 February. Robin was in despair. 'I wish to make it clear in all humility', he said, 'that when one begins to think that one understands the position in Northern Ireland, that is the time to start all over again. Although I am of Northern Ireland, I have started all over again many times.' While he lamented the deaths of his constituents, he attacked the way the IRA was intimidating large parts of Londonderry, expressed his concern that nothing should be done to inhibit the troops from defending themselves or law-abiding citizens or from taking the initiative against the IRA, and questioned why an illegal march had taken place at all. He asked his fellow MPs to remember that 'there are thousands upon thousands of law-abiding citizens of Northern Ireland who will never, as long as they live, forget the courage and humanity shown by both the police and the troops in the last two years or more'. He stressed once again his consistency in promoting the need for change in the province, saying, 'I was the first person and the most frequent to say over and over again that the answer to discrimination in Northern Ireland was to provide houses and jobs, that, while there was a shortage of both, there would never be an end to discrimination.' He concluded with a plea for private roundtable talks involving all sides. Robin, however, was followed first by Bernadette Devlin, second by Ian Paisley, whose contributions epitomised the extreme views held on opposite sides of the divide, views that were crowding out the moderate views of traditional Unionists like Robin.[15]

---

14 *A Tragedy of Errors*, Kenneth Bloomfield, p25
15 Hansard, Northern Ireland, 1 Feb 1972, cols 285–92

In articles Robin wrote in the aftermath of Bloody Sunday, there is a trace of bitterness in his assertion that not one of the grievances raised by Northern Ireland's minority community was 'worth a shot fired in anger'. He attacked civil disobedience, which, he said, 'rankles with the majority just as internment with the minority'. He criticised John Hume for constantly adding to the movement's grievances as soon as others had been dealt with and for his abstention, with his colleagues, from Stormont. What, he concluded, was the point of reform if those for whom reform was implemented refused to participate?[16]

At Westminster Ulster Unionists met the Prime Minister on 29 February 1972. Notes prepared by Stratton Mills show that Ted Heath was likely to impose direct rule over Northern Ireland, transferring responsibility for *all* security matters to the British Government. He suggested that the number of Northern Ireland MPs might be increased to compensate for the end of devolution. News of the meeting reached Brian Faulkner, who wrote a scolding letter to Robin on 8 March. 'I think it most regrettable that at a time when so-called "political initiatives" are very much in the air, there should appear to be a willingness on the part of the Ulster Members to contemplate changes – even long-term – in the Northern Ireland Constitution.' Reminding Robin that support for the constitution was part of the rules and constitution of the Ulster Unionist Council, he asked for a meeting to clear the air. Robin's response was understandably curt, rejecting a meeting and underlining that he had made it clear to Heath on behalf of all his colleagues that 'whatever members might think about the long-term future, none of them believed any

16 CCLK3/4 *Birmingham Post, East Anglian Daily Times, Sunday Express,* press cuttings

action should be taken which put in question the future of the Stormont Parliament'. Regardless of what Ulster Unionists said to Heath, the odds on direct rule were shortening, as Robin knew, and he frequently tried to impress this on Brian Faulkner. As he later wrote,

> it was quite impossible not to divine what was going on and Faulkner had been warned by more than a few of apparently impending events. As Chairman, at that moment, of the Ulster Unionist members at Westminster, I was asked and expected to liaise with Northern Ireland's Prime Minister. I did so and twice rang him at his home in Co Down to warn him of what I believed was likely to occur. He insisted that he had assurances to the contrary and was immovable.[17]

* * *

On Friday 24 March 1972 Ted Heath announced that direct rule would be imposed from the end of the month and that he was appointing Willie Whitelaw as the first Secretary of State for Northern Ireland. The decision exposed rifts within the Ulster Unionists. While Robin was receptive to the announcement, commenting that complete integration within the UK would have been preferable, his colleague Willie Orr objected strongly, describing direct rule as 'an act of folly'. This was effectively Robin's last major contribution in the Commons on the subject of Northern Ireland. During the subsequent debate in the following week on the necessary legislation,

17 CCLK3/14 Faulkner to RCC, 8 Mar 1972, and personal notes made by RCC. Note: Robin had been elected chairman of the UU group in November 1971 in succession to Willie Orr

he limited himself to a number of brief interventions, for instance, extolling the Royal Ulster Constabulary as one of the world's finest police forces, or seeking assurances that the guarantees given about the border in the 1949 Act would remain in place. Stratton Mills had considered it strange that at a specially convened meeting of the 1922 Committee held in advance of the debate on Monday 27 March, Robin declined to speak on direct rule, asking Stratton to do so instead.

Within a few days the reason would become clear. On the Sunday evening Robin had been asked to see the Prime Minister in Downing Street. He was told to enter not through the front door but through the garden gate from Horse Guards Parade. Robin found his friend on his own. After saying good evening, Heath, recalled Robin, 'then maintained one of his longest and most disconcerting silences'. When he broke his silence, the purpose of the meeting became clear: Ted was finally honouring his promise to offer Robin a ministerial appointment. In doing so, however, he betrayed once more the lack of understanding about Northern Ireland that so dismayed Robin, offering him a junior ministerial role in the new Northern Ireland Office. This was out of the question, Robin told him, since his acceptance would be seen as treacherous by many in Northern Ireland, on either side of the community divide, making his appointment as good as useless. Instead, he accepted the post of Minister of State for Employment. The announcement was not made until early April when Maurice Macmillan, son of the Prime Minister under whom Robin had served as a whip, was appointed as Secretary of State for Employment; Robin's acceptance accounted for his reticence on the subject of Northern Ireland during the intervening period.[18]

---

18 Hansard, Northern Ireland, 24 Mar 1972, col 1870; Parliament, RCC

Robin did, however, take the trouble to put down on paper his thoughts about the future of the province, which he sent to his brother James, now Lord Moyola. His experience of Northern Ireland politics had convinced him, he wrote, that 'there must never again be a system with even the powers of a "devolved" government and that any assembly must never be called a Parliament. It goes without saying that there cannot be a "Prime Minister".' The existing system, which he had defended loyally for so long, he blamed for creating an innately divided community, the majority constantly on the defensive, increasingly aggressive, feeling under threat from all sides. The fortress mentality this created, Robin felt, was exacerbated by the province's physical separation from the mainland and by the creation of a devolved 'Parliament' and 'Government' which ignored what was going on at Westminster. As Robin had always regretted, the population, he wrote, 'turned in upon themselves, became preoccupied with their own affairs and forgot a wider world'. At Stormont there were too many MPs too easily influenced by the province's cultural institutions, such as the Orange Order: 'Britain had created a breeding ground for moral and indeed physical cowardice.' When it was clear that the status quo was no longer tenable, the permanent Unionist majority at Stormont proved unequal to the pressure: 'as a result, the majority party was torn with dissension, and for every step taken by men like O'Neill and Moyola towards the healing of community wounds, there were other Unionist or Protestant leaders who cried "betrayal" or "appeasement", which found echo among the many who had been conditioned to the fortress mentality'.[19]

Robin's views were not typical of his Unionist colleagues.

---

19 CCLK3/14, Copy of paper sent by RCC to his brother

Most of them found it impossible to welcome direct rule. It was the fissure that split the long-standing relationship between the Ulster Unionists and the Conservatives. On 30 March 1972 the eight-strong group, still chaired by Robin, voted by a majority to withhold general support from the Government and give no further notice of the group's voting intentions. The announcement of Robin's ministerial appointment a week later only widened the gap. Robin's justification of his acceptance in the context of the imposition of direct rule incensed many of his fellow Unionists: arguing that Ulster's politicians prior to partition had always believed the province should be governed from London like any other part of the UK, Robin was taking up his post 'to demonstrate my belief that the fundamental strength of unionism is full participation in the United Kingdom'.[20]

Northern Ireland's press gave Robin's appointment as minister of state a mixed reception. He was still one of the youngest members of the Government and his ability was not in doubt; *The Times* believed it was 'not only a tactful appointment in the present circumstances but also one that is justified in personal terms'. Writing in *The Spectator*, however, Hugh MacPherson commented that his promotion was 'an act of gross cynicism' that had removed 'a dangerous influence among the rebellious Ulster MPs', concluding that 'it is the swiftest seduction since Don Juan abandoned women and took to late-night feasting and stone statues'. Ireland's *Sunday Independent* was spot on, however, when it remarked that Robin had become 'the most unpopular man in Unionist circles', observing that his 'political somersault has not only angered his closest colleagues, it has put his whole future as a politician in jeopardy. It seems virtually certain, judging by

---

20 CCLK3/14 RCC's statement on joining the Government, April 1972

first reactions, that he will not be renominated by his Derry constituency.' In a sign of just how far politics in Northern Ireland had changed, Robin's constituency party passed a vote of no confidence in him, in sharp contrast to the congratulations he had received when he became a whip all those years before.[21]

Robin would spend less than two years as a minister. One of his greatest satisfactions came from helping to further moves towards equal employment legislation; he had always been a supporter of equal opportunities for women. Robin's son Mark would stay with him at his flat in Wilton Row where a feature of life was 'the lovely Molly who would turn up in the morning in a large sleek ministerial car and ferry Robin off to the House of Commons or the Department of Employment in St James's Square. She was a lovely person and I enjoyed catching a ride with them whenever I could.' It was not an easy job for Robin. He was always less confident speaking in the Commons on matters he felt he knew less about and employment was one of them. Moreover, the Conservative Government found itself embroiled in all sorts of industrial disputes, with strikes occurring frequently, and the Department of Employment played a significant role. At the same time, Robin's personal life was difficult and he was still visiting his constituency most weeks, where the violence was continuing to worsen. He was appalled when Willie Whitelaw informed the House of Commons in early July 1972 that he had met leaders of the Provisional IRA in secret following the short-lived truce they had declared in the wake of the imposition of direct rule. The talks were abortive and Whitelaw was heavily criticised. Robin came close to resigning. In a letter

---

21 CCLK 6/8/1 *The Times*, 8 Apr 1972, *The Spectator*, 15 Apr 1972, and the *Sunday Independent*, 16 Apr 1972; Garnett and Aitken, p113

to the Chief Whip Francis Pym on 11 July he described the meeting as 'distasteful' and 'the height of folly', stating that he would resign if the Cabinet discussed the IRA's demands. Three days later a letter arrived from Willie Whitelaw, telling Robin he understood his position and there was no question of accepting any IRA demands. As a postscript, in his own hand, Whitelaw had written, 'I know how you feel about the IRA meeting. <u>Don't you do anything.</u> If anyone has to, I will.'[22]

Scarcely a fortnight later, once the IRA had abandoned its truce, Robin was deeply affected by the bombing in the small village of Claudy in his constituency on 31 July 1972. Three car bombs went off in the village's main street in the middle of the morning when it was busy with shoppers. Nine people were killed in the attack, which became known as Bloody Monday. There was strong evidence to suggest that the local Catholic priest was involved, evidence that did not surface for nearly 40 years. When Robin was asked about his feelings for the IRA nearly 30 years later, he wrote,

> As someone who stood by the beds of the dying from the bombed and innocent village of Claudy where the two religions had enjoyed outstandingly friendly relationships, my feelings may be coloured. Proximity to people in that village and later in Coleraine, both Protestant and Catholic, their bodies violated and broken by bombs, clinging to life by their finger nails or oxygen tubes, does not at that time, or even 30 years on, help one to reach rational conclusions.[23]

As his PPS, Robin chose from the list presented to him

---

22 Personal Papers, RCC to Francis Pym, 11 Jul 1972; CCLK 1/10 Whitelaw to RCC, 14 Jul 1972
23 Personal Papers, RCC to Mark Garnett, 19 Aug 2001

Norman Tebbit, who had joined the Commons in 1970. It was Norman's first government post. 'Robin was very generous to me,' he recalled. 'He didn't just use me as his bag carrier; he took me a lot into the Department.' This gave Norman an understanding of the Department which proved helpful when he himself became Secretary of State for Employment under Margaret Thatcher. Norman recognised that it was not the best of times for Robin, observing that 'he was ill at ease in many ways'. He used his growing ministerial workload as an excuse not to visit Northern Ireland; in fact, on occasion he would send Norman himself to attend meetings of his Derry constituency association. In the aftermath of the end of Robin's first marriage, Norman would often invite him to dine with his wife Margaret and his children at their flat in the Barbican. Robin's fund of funny Irish stories made him a favourite with the Tebbit children. In a letter to Robin towards the end of his life, Norman wrote, 'I am only too happy to think that Margaret and I may have helped you, Robin, in your dark days. That is what friends are for.'[24]

Grey Gowrie, the 2nd Earl of Gowrie, was attached to the Department as a whip in the House of Lords. He had first met Robin some years before in Ted Heath's Albany rooms when Ted was Leader of the Opposition. Grey had taken an immediate liking to Robin but their paths had rarely crossed in the intervening period. Grey recalled how immersed the Department was in the major controversies over industrial relations and attempts to regulate trade union activities. He too remembered how Robin 'was an absent and rather ill figure' and during his absence Grey stood in for him. (Grey would hold the same position in the same department for almost the same length of time in Margaret Thatcher's first

24 Personal Papers, Norman Tebbit to RCC, 16 Apr 2016

government before moving to the Northern Ireland Office as Minister of State in 1981.) The two men got on well together. 'We bonded: he was very funny,' said Grey, 'and I liked him a lot.' They had much in common. For 20 years Grey's home had been in Ulster, albeit beyond the political boundaries of the province, in County Donegal, which looked to London-derry as its natural capital. His family had always known the Chichester-Clarks (or the 'Chi-Chesters', as they called them, rhyming 'Chi' with 'tie'), as they were tangentially part of Grey's mother and stepfather's circle. Grey had even met the formidable Dame Dehra when she came to fish at Dunlewy, Grey's Donegal home. Later, Grey and his wife would come to know Robin's first wife Jane and her second husband Paddy when the Gowries bought a home close by them in County Kildare. Grey understood the trajectory of Robin's political career, appreciating how he had moved from a traditional Orange Unionist background towards 'a much more pluralist and ecumenical view' of Ireland. He also understood that this journey had required Robin to play 'his cards quite close to his chest; he was cautious, he had to be'.

Another friend was Robin's personal assistant, Caroline Bull. She had previously spent some time in the Conserva-tive Research Department and began working for Robin, largely attending to his constituency correspondence, in the late summer of 1970 when she was just 23. Knowing nothing about him, his family or Unionist politics, she rang him at Ross House to say she was taking up the post. 'His first words to me were, "Oh! Could you bear to?" And I thought what a very nice thing to say.' When they met for the first time on the return of Parliament in October 1970, they struck up an immediate rapport. They discovered, for example, a shared passion for birdwatching. They watched kestrels nesting in the Victoria Tower of the House of Lords, and when Robin was at home in his constituency and rang his Westminster office, he would hold his receiver out of the window so Caroline could hear the curlews calling. She had no idea Robin's marriage was in trouble and was amazed to hear from him in 1971 that he was getting divorced. 'It never occurred to me that there was anything amiss and I never spotted anything was wrong at all.' By the summer of the following year, like Norman Tebbit, she could see that Robin was exhausted by Northern Ireland, his constituency, his ministerial duties, his divorce and keeping his family together. Having been to Marrakech twice, raising funds for the Leonard Cheshire home there, she recommended a hotel to Robin, suggesting it was the ideal place to get away from all his anxieties. On his return he would write to Willie Whitelaw how he had enjoyed 'lying in the hot sun in Marrakesh'.[25]

Perhaps the sunshine helped Robin to place his political prospects in perspective. His absence from constituency association meetings (partly because he refused to share a platform with members of Bill Craig's fascist Vanguard movement) caused his association to ask him in late November 1972 whether he would again be seeking the nomination for his seat. By the beginning of December, Robin had decided he would not. His disillusion with Northern Ireland politics was shared by his friend Stratton Mills, who declared his intention to sit as an independent Unionist and later joined the recently formed Alliance party. Robin's friend, the Labour MP Ray Carter, had begun to understand the pressure he was under only after the furore surrounding Robin's attendance at Conolly McCausland's funeral. He quite understood Robin's predicament, as did others in the House: the trouble Robin had dealing with his constituency association was a topic of

25 CCLK 3/14 RCC to Whitelaw, 17 Oct 1972

conversation. Ray recognised that Robin stood quite apart from the bigotry shown by too many Unionists in Ray's experience: 'Robin was a sensitive man and he wasn't part of that mentality. He was such a decent person but many of his colleagues were so bigoted we wondered how he had survived.'

Robin made his formal announcement that he would not be standing again for his Londonderry seat at the beginning of January 1973. The newspapers in the province agreed that Robin might have found considerable opposition among party members to his renomination. *The Irish Press*, in criticising Brian Faulkner for what it regarded as his misplaced criticism of Robin, presciently observed how 'the downward trend of [Faulkner's] inherited brand of Unionism is unmistakable'. Writing to Robin soon after his announcement, Sir Basil McFarland, Londonderry's Lord Lieutenant, noted that 'we could not blame you for we know only too well that your political life has been made hell in this constituency for the past two or three years'.[26]

During his last year, said Norman Tebbit, Robin came to dislike his ministerial brief: as the Heath Government's industrial strategy collapsed, he hated having to defend in the Commons what he considered to be indefensible. Although he would remain a friend of Ted Heath's, Robin became disillusioned with his leadership, seeing in his poor relationship with his own MPs shades of Terence O'Neill. Tebbit too was discontented, resigning his position in November 1973, writing to Robin, 'in a way I feel a bit of a rotten sod leaving when it looks like a rough ride ahead but perhaps I can be more useful on the back benches'. By then, the Heath Government was facing the crisis that would eventually bring it

26 CCLK 6/9 *The Irish Press*, 11 Jan 1973; CCLK 1/20 Sir Basil McFarland to RCC, 11 Jan 1973

down, as the miners imposed an overtime ban, leading to the so-called Three Day Week in December to conserve fuel supplies. Maurice Macmillan was replaced and Robin's old friend Willie Whitelaw was sent in as a troubleshooter to try and resolve matters.[27]

Robin had discussed his decision to quit his Ulster seat with Norman Tebbit. Norman recognised that the seat 'was no longer a natural match for him'. It was Norman who encouraged Robin to try to stay in politics, suggesting he should seek a Conservative seat in England. The idea appealed to Robin and it was partly for this reason that he declined the offer of a peerage from Ted Heath. He also rejected the idea because if he accepted Ted wanted him to set up the Conservative party in Northern Ireland. That would be impossible, he told the Prime Minister; putting up Conservative candidates could only split the Unionist vote. Once more Robin was astounded at Ted's lack of understanding. It distressed him to think that in all the years they had worked closely together he had been unable to get across to Ted the realities of politics in the province. As he later wrote, Heath 'was to the very end no better at seeing through to the core of Northern Ireland's problems than his predecessors'. Having turned down a peerage, Robin instead accepted a knighthood, which was included in the resignation honours lists following Heath's defeat in the February 1974 General Election. (With his poetic imagination and sense of humour, Robin had toyed with ideas for titles had he been ennobled, such as Lord Glenshane of the Sperrins, Lord Loughinsholin of the Kellswater or Lord Tamniarn, all Irish names of places he knew and loved.)

In his formal announcement that he was standing down from his Londonderry seat, Robin did express the wish to

---

27 CCLK 1/11 Norman Tebbit to RCC, 9 Nov 1973

continue in politics. He was expected to be able to find a safe Conservative seat on the mainland in time for the next General Election. He did not. When he failed to win the nomination for Lewes in January 1973, he had apparently impressed the selection committee, but there were concerns that as a political high-flyer he would not make a good constituency MP. This was ironic, first since Robin was acknowledged on all sides in his Londonderry seat as a hard-working and conscientious MP, and second since the chosen candidate, Tim Rathbone, was neither a good constituency MP nor a high-flyer. But the secretary of the local Conservative association suggested there was also another reason for Robin's failure, writing that 'I have a feeling that all the unavoidable newspaper publicity did not help.' Robin's Unionist past would prove a hindrance to his further ambitions: no English constituency wanted a candidate on an IRA death list. During the course of the year he also failed to gain the nomination for the South Norfolk seat. His failure to win selection was not only down to Northern Ireland. The stress he was under at several different levels, believed Norman Tebbit, meant he was only ever half-hearted in his pursuit of another seat. Moreover, he had little time from his ministerial duties in a department dealing with a major industrial crisis to gallivant around the country glad-handing constituency chairmen. He would make one more attempt in between the two 1974 elections, applying for the Dorset West seat, without success. 'I was always surprised', said Stratton Mills, 'that Robin was never offered some worthwhile role in public life.' The premature end to Robin's political career, however, should not detract from the contribution he had made with considerable courage in difficult circumstances in bringing about change in Northern Ireland, nor from his principled adherence to a moderate, non-sectarian view of politics in the province. The tragedy was that by the time Robin left Ulster politics there was precious little room left for moderation.[28]

---

28 CCLK 1/20 Letter from Lewes Division Conservative Association to RCC, 19 Jan 1973

PART THREE

A NEW LIFE

CHAPTER SIX

MARRIAGE, FAMILY AND FRIENDS

By the time Robin's political career reached a premature end, he had already embarked on the second phase of his life. For Robin, that was marked by his marriage to Caroline Bull on 9 January 1974, which lasted until his death more than 42 years later.

Robin and Caroline had grown closer following Robin's divorce in 1972. In the autumn of 1973, he proposed. Caroline hesitated. She was part-way through her studies for the Bar and wanted to wait until she had completed her finals in the summer of 1974. She was already in love with Robin but didn't quite know what to do. With an age gap of nearly 20 years, Caroline was worried about how Robin's children would respond, even though she had met them all when she spent a fortnight with them in Northern Ireland in the summer of 1973. What she probably didn't realise was how much Robin's children already liked her. It was during that summer break in Ulster that the children realised just how close Robin and Caroline had become. 'To us three children,' said Mark Chichester-Clark,

Caroline made an enormous difference. We were very excited when she turned up. Before they had told us they were closer than just friends, I can remember walking behind them through one of the little coastal towns [Cushendun] and seeing his hand reach for hers and then, realising we were behind him, pulling it back. Emma and Fia and I all looked at each other with some delight. It really did cheer him and bring him out of himself and it certainly cheered us up: we would write her little notes telling her how much we liked her.

Meeting her for the first time that summer, said Emma, 'was a great relief because she was easy to get on with and we all liked her. She was young and fun and fitted in and [Robin] was cheerful.' In time Caroline grew to love all three.

The memory of this kindness and friendliness helped Caroline to make up her mind as she was thinking over Robin's proposal.

I felt that if they were friendly, then I could perhaps do it. I thought I could make him laugh, make him happy, help to get his life together again. I'm sure he would have got himself together but at that moment he was feeling pretty destroyed by everything. You can imagine that if your job has gone wrong, if your country has gone wrong, if your marriage has gone wrong, it was tough.

Caroline was in no doubt that she loved Robin. Irreverent but not unkind, he was tall, good-looking and charming, with piercing blue eyes, a very warm, deep, resonant voice and a mischievous, slightly wicked smile. But she admits she wobbled because of her impending finals. Robin's sister Penelope helped her to make up her mind; Caroline asked her if she thought marrying Robin was a sensible thing to do. In her characteristically forthright way, Penelope told Caroline that of course it was sensible – Robin loved her – she should get on with it.

Her father was less enthusiastic. Anthony Bull had made a

successful career with London Transport, eventually becoming vice-chairman. His own father, Caroline's grandfather, Sir William Bull, had been the flamboyant Conservative MP for Hammersmith from 1900 until 1929. Anthony was third of four brothers, all witty and intelligent, two of whom joined the family law firm, Bull & Bull, the other, Peter, becoming an actor. Like Robin, Anthony Bull had been at Magdalene College, Cambridge, where he knew well and greatly admired Robin's uncle, Francis Clark. After graduating he spent his entire career with London Transport.

He married Barbara Donovan in October 1946. He was 38 and she was 24. The daughter of an Irish-Canadian father, a writer who had come to England with Max Aitken, later Lord Beaverbrook, and an English mother, Barbara was strikingly beautiful. The couple had met during the war when Barbara, serving in the Women's Royal Naval Service, joined Mountbatten's staff at his headquarters in Kandy, Ceylon, in 1943. Anthony, who was organising supply routes for the British troops, was also based in Kandy.

Caroline was born in July 1947 but her mother died just three months later from polio while on holiday in North Wales. Her father remained a widower until his death 57 years later. She remembered 'he was a very good parent, trying to be both father and mother'. She gained from him a love of travel as she accompanied him to international transport conferences and on one occasion a visit to Japan and the USA in 1967 to shop for the first automatic ticket gates for the London Underground. She also visited Ireland where her maternal great-uncle, Peter Wilson, lived in Oranmore Castle in County Galway.[1] He knew and liked Robin's grandmother,

---

1 Colonel Peter Wilson commanded the Trans-Jordan Frontier Force from 1940 to 1946, and later served on Churchill's staff in Berlin and London. He

Dame Dehra, who he would meet while staying at Castle Leslie, Glaslough, in County Monaghan and at Glenveagh Castle, home of the American collector Henry McIlhenny, in County Donegal. Robin also met Peter at Glaslough. Peter used to take Caroline to search for gentians and orchids growing in the crevices between the limestone slabs in the Burren in County Clare, a part of Ireland Robin loved too. Caroline travelled widely on her own after leaving school, spending time in France and Italy. After leaving the Conservative Research Department she went out to Morocco to raise funds, largely from companies in Casablanca, for the Leonard Cheshire home in Marrakech, the Foyer Koutoubia, which looked after children who had suffered from polio. Her closest friend in Marrakech was Sir Claude Auchinleck, the distinguished field marshal who had commanded the Eighth Army in Egypt during the Second World War, who was then in his eighties. They went on expeditions, or took picnics, into the Atlas Mountains and often had dinner together. It was on her return that she became Robin's personal assistant.

When Caroline told her father about Robin's proposal, he thought she was mad to think of marrying an older man with three children; he would later tell her he felt he was gaining another father rather than losing a daughter. Caroline resisted pointing out to her father the difference in ages between him and her mother. Anthony, however, became very fond of Robin, discovering they had a great deal in common.

Robin wanted the marriage to take place before his 46th birthday on 10 January 1974 so the couple booked the Crypt of the House of Commons for a service of blessing on Wednesday 9 January following a registry office ceremony

---

met the writer Anita Leslie in Palestine where she had volunteered as an ambulance driver and they began a lifelong relationship.

TOP: Caroline, Robin's second wife, 1973 BOTTOM: Robin and Caroline's
wedding, 9 January 1974

TOP: James and Moyra Moyola BOTTOM: Mark, Fia and Emma. Caroline's father and Robin in the background

TOP LEFT: Emma TOP RIGHT: Fia BOTTOM: Mark with springer spaniel, Fergus, at Ross House

TOP LEFT: Caroline, Tom and Robin striding out on the Burnham Norton Marshes in Norfolk TOP RIGHT: Caroline BOTTOM LEFT: Robin with Tom and Adam BOTTOM RIGHT: Tom

TOP LEFT: Tom with Emma at Yarlington TOP RIGHT: Adam's wedding, North Cadbury, Somerset, September 2008 BOTTOM: Emma, Tom, Finn, Sam, Mark, Nina, Adam, Will, Fia with Maudie the springer spaniel

TOP LEFT: Robin at Moyola TOP RIGHT: Philip Goodhart BOTTOM LEFT: Robin and Caroline as Talleyrand and the Duchess of Dino at Charles de Salis's Napoleonic 50th birthday ball BOTTOM RIGHT: Robin as the Bishop of Carlisle in *Richard II* with Tom Stuart-Smith

TOP: Diana Rigg, Seamus Heaney, Imogen Stubbs and Ted Hughes at the Garrick after a poetry reading MIDDLE: Grey Gowrie BOTTOM: Robin with Seamus Heaney at the Art Workers' Guild

Grandpa 1928-2016

TOP: Robin in the woods at Moyola BOTTOM: Emma's portrait of Robin with his dogs recorded by her dog, Plum

at Caxton Hall. 'MP marries law student,' said one London newspaper. The reception was supposed to take place in the House of Commons dining room. 'We were going to have 350 people', said Caroline, 'and ask everybody we knew. But by then we were into the Three Day Week and all sorts of political troubles and there was an emergency recall of the House of Commons, and they needed their dining room, so that put paid to our reception there.' Instead, thanks to Robin's brother, now in the Lords, they were able to use the Cholmondeley Room; the drawback was that it held only 200 people and the couple were asked to invite even fewer than that. 'My father said as it was his last party, he wasn't cancelling any of his friends and he was paying for it, so I cancelled half my friends and Robin cancelled all his friends.' Caroline was also upset that the church had told them that no more than 20 people should attend the service of blessing, otherwise it might look like a remarriage; in the event, she managed to get away with squeezing in 80. But there was a magical quality to the afternoon, for after the civil ceremony, Caroline remembered, 'we walked across Parliament Square as it grew dark, the lights came on and snow began to fall'.

The couple began their married life in London, initially in Robin's Wilton Row flat, moving soon afterwards into the basement flat of Anthony Bull's house in Pelham Place, one of South Kensington's elegant Regency terraces. In November 1974 they bought their first house in Fulham, followed four years later by the second, in one of the so-called Alphabet Streets, running between the Thames and Fulham Palace Road. Their first son, Adam, was born in 1975 and their second, Tom, in 1976. Robin wasn't really an urban dweller, but the house in Ellerby Street would become a comfortable home for the whole family. As one friend, Anthea Carver, recalled, 'I don't think he was the right person for Fulham but he made the best of it.' Robin appreciated the proximity of Bishop's Park. So too did Fergus, his springer spaniel. More used to roaming the hills of County Antrim, Fergus never totally adjusted to life in London, and if the front door was open he would dash down to the lake in the park and chase the ducks.

At heart, Robin was a countryman. Although he was at ease socially in London, he was happiest walking with his dogs in the country or watching birds, and Moyola was the place he most loved. When the opportunity came to acquire a country property, Robin and Caroline took it. In August 1974 Robin severed his permanent links with Ulster when Ross House was sold. His sister Penelope, living at Hadspen House in Somerset, suggested they should look at a house for sale in nearby Yarlington. With Mark, Caroline drove down to see it and liked it. Big enough for the whole family, with a large garden, the dower house for Yarlington House was in a quiet village and surrounded by woodland and fields. Caroline rang Robin in London who told her to go ahead if she thought it would do and that his big Irish bookcases would fit. She shook hands with Charles de Salis, later a great friend, who was selling the house, and the deal was done.

Yarlington became a wonderful refuge for the whole family and Robin loved spending time there. He was probably happiest when he and Caroline were surrounded by their family at Yarlington. His son Adam remembered the comfort of being on his father's knee in the sitting room beside the fire, cosy on dark, damp winter nights, or watching the rugby internationals, with Adam cheering for England and his father for Ireland. And there were games, all sorts of games, card games, board games, charades, which Robin loved to play, always playing to win. There Robin learned to relax. He no longer had any need to be secretive, allowing him to let down his guard and be himself.

Robin and Caroline settled very quickly into village life, making a completely new set of friends. 'It was', said John Wiseman, 'a friendship you could see and smell and taste.' The Wisemans, John and Sarah, lived just over the hill from Yarlington. 'I knew Robin', said John, 'as a man and a friend whom I loved very much.' While John came in for some gentle teasing from Robin because he was American, it was never offensive. 'He was never carried away by his own social position,' said John. 'There was always a modesty about him … He was not just likeable, he was loveable. He was a friend, he was a pal, you could go into battle with him and you knew he would never let you down.' Across the road from The Rookery lived Charles and Tineke Pugh, while Charles and Carolyn de Salis, who had sold the house to Robin and Caroline, lived further up the road. 'You couldn't really fail to fall in love with Robin,' said Charles Pugh. 'He was a most lovely man.' Robin, said Carolyn de Salis, 'loved company and being with people.'

His neighbours soon discovered Robin's passion for the countryside. Charles Pugh readily agreed to Robin's request that since his meadows harboured voles as prey for the tawny owls, they should remain uncut for as long as possible. It was Charles who wrote an anonymous letter to *The Spectator*'s problem-solving page describing how Robin had bought two owl whistles, giving one to his neighbour, Rodney Cotton, an equally passionate birdwatcher. Unbeknown to one another, they went out at dusk, each blowing their whistle in turn, each convinced they were winning replies from nearby owls. As Charles Pugh wrote, 'It is quite clear that these two gentlemen have been hooting to each other, with no actual owl involved.'

In the village, where Robin always joined in with fundraising events, such as the appeal for the church roof, he was a calming influence, good at bringing people together, persuading them to talk to one another and forget their foibles. Robin was asked to chair the church roof appeal committee, which he handled with customary aplomb. He was, said his friend James Buxton, 'the most wonderful chairman of meetings: he had the ability to apply his charm in the most productive way; but it wasn't just charm, it was good judgement too'. Robin's political skills rarely deserted him.

Friendship was a fundamental part of Robin's life. The friends he made usually lasted a lifetime; the exceptions, such as Terence O'Neill, were rare. Despite his disappointment in Ted Heath, Robin stayed in touch with him until Ted's death in 2005. They liked each other and Robin was one of the few people who could gently puncture Ted's pomposity. He was never cowed by Ted and rarely discomforted by him. Once Robin and Caroline had settled in Somerset and Ted had retired to Salisbury, they were often invited to join him for lunch. Always informally dressed, Ted would greet his friends on the steps of his beautiful house in the Cathedral Close. Champagne in hand, they would walk down to the confluence of the rivers at the bottom of his garden, with Ted pointing out what had been planted that summer. He was a generous host and loved to see people enjoying themselves. He never lost his quirkiness: when Robin and Caroline lunched with him on their own, he had a tendency to expect them to sit in silence post-luncheon through one of his own recordings, such as his conducting of Beethoven's *Triple Concerto*.

Another long-standing friendship was with Philip Goodhart, whom Robin had met as a young man during his time in the USA. Philip's father was an American who spent his academic career in England, where he was for many years professor of jurisprudence at Oxford. Later the first American to become master of an Oxford college, he was subsequently awarded an honorary KBE. Philip's grandmother Harriet (known as Hattie) was the daughter of Mayer Lehman, one of the founders of Lehman Brothers, whose failure many years later was the harbinger of the collapse of financial markets around the world. By then the family was no longer involved in running the bank. Philip was born in England but studied in the USA before winning a place at Cambridge in 1950. He became MP for Beckenham in Kent in 1957, two years after Robin joined the Commons, and their friendship grew closer over the years. Politically, they had much in common. Philip too had a strong sense of public service, believed in looking after his constituents, supported the Unionist cause in Northern Ireland and was moderate in his opinions. As the long-standing joint secretary of the 1922 Committee, he was involved in the election of Ted Heath to the leadership in 1965, when Robin was one of Ted's most active supporters. Like Robin, Philip was knighted for political service. Robin became godfather to Philip's son David and Philip became godfather to Emma. Robin and Caroline, sometimes with their two boys, spent many happy weekends at Whitebarn on Boar's Hill, the Goodharts' house just outside Oxford, which had belonged to Philip's father. Philip died in 2015, a year before Robin.

Robin's connections with the Stuart-Smith family also went back a long way. Robin had met Murray Stuart-Smith at Cambridge and the two families spent several holidays together on the County Donegal coast. The friendship survived Robin's divorce and gained new strength when Robin married Caroline. The shared holidays continued, this time overseas, to destinations such as Spain and Czechoslovakia. The latter visit took place soon after the end of the Cold War, when the shops were still largely bare. Murray strongly disapproved of Robin and Caroline taking rolls from breakfast to save for their lunch until he discovered for himself how little food was available outside the hotel. There were family concerts at the Stuart-Smiths' home, Serge Hill, and the outdoor perfor-mances of Shakespeare once performed on top of Donegal's cliffs now took place in the Stuart-Smiths' garden on a grass stage with clipped yew wings designed by their son, Tom. For many years the two couples attended innumerable opera performances together, in London and at Glyndebourne and Garsington. Murray liked Robin because 'of a coincidence of ideas – we tended to think alike'. 'I remember that warm gravelly voice of his,' said Murray. 'He would ring me up and I would hear his very unmistakable voice.' Robin never had the reluctance of some people when faced with making a phone call. If he could not see people in person, he loved to ring them up and chat. When the phone rang in London or Somerset, he usually leapt to answer the call, and if he was not first, he would always ask who had called, what they wanted, and what news they had.

Robin, said Murray's daughter, Kate, 'was one of those people who are truly interested in you'. Not for Robin the gaze over people's shoulder seeking out a person of greater interest. He believed there was something interesting about almost everyone if you took the trouble to find out. 'Robin found people endlessly fascinating,' said Caroline, 'and he was a good listener.' 'He was somebody you could tell anything to,' said another of his friends, Jane Manley. Whenever he was out walking, he loved to stop and talk to people. He exuded a warmth that was tangible to everyone of all ages. Young chil-dren never hesitated to climb all over him and his nieces and grandchildren, including Luca, aged only four when Robin died, were very fond of him. He talked to them as equals regardless of any age difference and happily spent time with them. He was quick, for instance, to spot the interests of

Mark's children, Sam and Grace, when they spent time with him in Norfolk or Somerset. He sent Sam bird magazines to encourage his interest in ornithology, nicknaming him 'the Professor'. Fia remembered her cousins Tara, known as Bebe, and Fiona coming to stay. 'They always used to clamber onto my father's knee ... they saw their uncle as someone who would give them hugs and affection.' 'He was always interested in people, including my friends,' said his son Tom, 'and he would talk to people in a way that made them understand he was interested in them. Friends of mine loved my dad and found him hilarious; he achieved some kind of legendary status with them.' Long-lasting friendships brought him countless godchildren. Among them was Mark Stroyan, son of another of Robin's oldest friends, Angus Stroyan, a highly regarded circuit judge. As his godson, Mark said, one 'got the sense that [Robin] always cared about you'. Like so many of those who came within Robin's orbit, Mark felt that if he ever needed to, he could confide in Robin. He was, said Mark, 'an incredibly wise, thoughtful and constructive man – he never saw barriers, he always tried to find solutions'.

Robin made friends all his life. The school run was one catalyst for new friendships. This was how Robin and Caroline became friendly with Jeremy and Anthea Carver, who lived in an adjacent street in London, and how they cemented their friendship with Jane and Dickie Manley. The Manleys had become friends when Robin and Caroline holidayed at their hotel in Taormina, Sicily, in 1974 and when they returned to the UK, they too became near-neighbours of the Chichester-Clarks. Jane shared the school run with Robin and Caroline to their sons' pre-prep school at Eaton House. In an echo of Mark at Eton, Robin accompanied Adam into the school cloakroom on his first day to make sure Adam knew how to do up his sandals. They both knew he could but it was

Robin's way of making sure his son was happy in his new sur-roundings. Jeremy and Anthea Carver later took turns to take the boys, all of whom became friends, to their prep school at Colet Court.

With friends, however, who came into his life after he had given up his parliamentary seat, Robin rarely talked about Northern Ireland. It seemed clear, said Anthea Carver, that Robin had closed the door on that part of his life. Jane Manley too found that Robin would never talk about his political career, although he did tease her for her support of Margaret Thatcher, whom he never liked. This reticence was under-standable, and it was a feeling he shared with his brother James and with his daughters. Whenever Fia or Emma were asked about their experience of Northern Ireland, said Fia, 'we would say that we didn't know anything about it, we blocked it out. On social occasions – and it still happens today – when people would ask "What are your views on this?", a cloud would come down and we would claim no knowledge, because we had felt it so intensely through the arguments and through the tension our father felt, which cascaded down.' Although Robin would discuss the past with Caroline – images of the victims of the Claudy bombing often came back to him and Robin always regretted the absence of a political platform from which to express his views – he felt unable to bring himself to talk much about it with his two younger sons. Adam believed it was just too painful for his father, that despite everything he had done, he still felt guilty that his efforts had never been good enough.

Life beyond politics, most people who knew him agreed, treated Robin more kindly. And he was able to harness the skills he had developed in new directions. But he could not escape the impact of his political past easily. The accumulated stresses and strains of his time in active politics finally caught up with him not during the difficult years of the early 1970s but more than a decade later. The realisation came while he and Caroline were visiting Poland in the mid-1980s, staying with John Morgan, the British ambassador, and his wife Angela. Robin knew John well since John's first wife, Fionn O'Neill, was a distant relative. 'I first met John Morgan', Robin later recalled, 'shooting in County Antrim on a memorable occasion when Ian Fleming, his stepfather-in-law, did the "reprehensible" (shooting between drives) by downing a sky-high pheasant, already well past us, seemingly without turning his head. Any mention of James Bond thereafter recalled this incident and was a point of reference between us.' Robin also had been best man at John's marriage to his second wife, Angela Rathbone, who was one of Caroline's oldest school friends. The Chichester-Clarks travelled to Poland when the Communist status quo was under threat from the Solidarity movement. John warned Robin and Caroline that everything was bugged, the truth of which they discovered for themselves when they surprised the embassy's assistant butler changing the bug in their bedroom. John Morgan shared Robin's love of birdwatching and he took Robin to visit the Masurian Lakes close to the border with Russia. The Rector of Warsaw University went with them and on reaching the sanctuary at the lakes they enjoyed an extensive dinner, singing national songs well into the small hours, fuelled by ample vodka. Next morning, at dawn, with the Rector still soundly asleep, the British pair slipped out of the small wooden hut and headed for the reed beds where for the first time they were able to talk freely. They spotted 76 species, including white-tailed eagles.

Although Robin enjoyed his visit, he knew something was wrong with him, and on his return his doctor referred him to a consultant with experience of the impact on people of hostile environments. Depression was his diagnosis. Robin's daughter Fia wondered whether the misery of his years at Dartmouth might also have been a contributing factor. Another, Caroline believed, might have been that Robin had never had the chance to mourn the loss of his father properly. (They felt united by the loss of a parent in early childhood.) It was an anxious time for everyone in the family; it was, said Fia, her father's point of crisis and he was deeply unhappy. Mental illness was still a taboo subject and Robin insisted as few people should know as possible. He was prescribed medication, he took time off work and he exercised in the fresh air every day, usually in Richmond Park, accompanied by Caroline and Fergus, their springer spaniel. His recovery was gradual, assisted eventually by his charitable fundraising activities, which helped him to regain his confidence. He would suffer mild relapses for the rest of his life but this gave him an empathy for those in the same plight: he had, said Fia, 'a sensitivity to unhappiness'. Loyal, protective and supportive, Caroline, his children recognised, brought their father much-needed stability.

Marrying Caroline and distancing himself from Northern Ireland did help Robin to rebuild his relationship with his older children in the aftermath of his divorce from Jane. 'He changed quite a lot when he got married again,' recalled Emma. 'He relaxed. He became much more able to show his feelings – affection especially. He trusted us again.' He became, said Mark, very loyal to his children, thoughtful and solicitous, taking their side during difficult relationships, treating them all as equals, never talking down to them. Fia, just 13 when her father married again, found that being with Robin and Caroline helped her to see him as he really was rather than the distorted image seen through the lens of the divorce. 'For me,' said Fia, 'Caroline was the person who brought it all together again.' As she grew up, Fia found that she had much in common with her father, including the same sense of humour and the same desire to put people at their ease.

With the arrival of two sons, Robin also learned to be a father once more. No longer tied to the irregular hours and demanding commitments of a parliamentarian but keeping normal working hours for the first time since his early twenties, Robin delighted in coming home for supper in the evenings and reading to the boys at bedtime. Fia loved having two baby boys to look after but, said Emma, they 'were so naughty, even when they were little'. Staying at Ellerby Street while her own flat was being altered, Emma would come down in the morning to find these two youngsters, six and seven, using kitchen knives to have sword fights. 'They were very sweet but completely out of control. Their aunt Penny called them "the devils". They were dreadful but very funny and clever, always curious, always wanting to learn.' It was not easy for either Robin or Caroline. Part of the reason Robin made such a great effort the second time around was because he recognised he was a much older parent. He was determined to be as active a father as possible and he loved playing all sorts of games with the boys. There was a strange version of indoor football played upstairs at Ellerby Street and at Yarlington there were constant croquet, cricket and football matches.

Robin did his utmost to impart his passion for the countryside to his sons. 'This was a man', said Sarah Wiseman, 'who adored nature.' 'Although he accepted that we needed to be based in London for his work,' said Tom, 'he wanted us to have experienced the same country childhood that he had known.' Somerset gave Adam and Tom an equivalent opportunity to learn about the natural world as County Antrim and County Donegal had given to Emma, Mark and Fia. It seemed to Adam as a boy that the family travelled down to

Yarlington almost every weekend. His father fostered in both boys an instinctive love for the countryside, for birds, animals and plants. Both boys recalled Robin taking them on dark summer nights to the wood beside the house to sit behind the trees, upwind of the badger setts, where they waited for the badgers to come out and play. 'He made it the most exciting adventure of all,' said Tom. 'He wanted us to be as excited by nature as he was and it worked.' The boys would often stride off on long walks with their father. Robin also encouraged Adam when he was writing about nature for his school work, either an essay or a poem, which married Robin's two loves, literature and nature. He made sure the boys experienced the beauty of Moyola, where they fished on the river. On holiday in Portugal with Stratton Mills and his family, Robin took Tom to watch ospreys fishing and he pointed out the hoopoe flying over the swimming pool with its peach colouring and spectacular crest. In Majorca he wanted the boys to see the Eleonora's falcons diving through the air from the dramatic cliffs at Formentor on the north-eastern tip of the island. The tortuous drive to the cape, nerve-wracking at the best of times, was made more thrilling for the boys because their father kept only one hand on the wheel, using the other to point out birds in the sky, frightening their mother so much that she insisted on getting out of the car. Back in England, there were frequent visits to the coast around the Burnhams in Norfolk where Caroline's father owned a house in Burnham Norton. The Burnhams were one of Robin and Caroline's favourite places and they would get up early to watch the birds on the marshes.

Robin had loved history at Cambridge and this he also instilled in his two boys. Adam remembered his father reading chapters to him from Henrietta Marshall's classic child's history of England, *Our Island Story*. There was a

Swan Hellenic cruise around the Aegean where the boys were thrilled to stand on the walls of Troy in the early-morning sunlight and listen to one lecturer give a rendering of Hector's last speech in ancient Greek, followed by the same account in English. In Mexico, where the family stayed with John and Angela Morgan, when John was ambassador there, they travelled to the pyramids of Teotihuacán, near Mexico City, and Chichen Itza and Uxmal on the Yucatán Peninsula.

The boys, close together in age, formed a strong bond early on, and they were upset when their parents decided to send Tom to a different prep school from his brother. While Adam went to Colet Court, Tom went to board at Summerfields. Boarding school life, felt his parents, would suit him better as a boy who was easily distracted and often procrastinated when faced with homework. For a year Tom was desperately homesick. Whenever the time came for him to return to school by coach, 'there were traumatic scenes … I was totally distraught and often there were tears. It was all incredibly tense and dramatic; it felt like being ripped away from the family.' At the end of the summer holidays in his first year, Tom climbed up the apple tree in the garden and refused to come down, throwing apples at anyone who came near. Tom did not go back to Summerfields, joining his brother at Colet Court instead.

By and large, said Caroline, the first 15 years of marriage were 'cloudless'. Whatever naughtiness the boys got up to was manageable. Things became more challenging when the boys were teenagers. Although they both won places to Eton, they elected to remain at St Paul's as day boys. There were few constraints since their mother, said Adam, never really believed in discipline, their father was not in the best of health and none of this was helped by Caroline's own bout of illness. The boys also began to appreciate that their father was much older than the fathers of most of their peers. Tom freely admits that he ran wild, mixing with youngsters up to no good in the local park, taking advantage of his father's more relaxed approach to him as his youngest child. Often truanting from school, he got into debt by obtaining a credit card when he was underage. His father repeatedly came to his rescue. 'He was forever getting me out of the scrapes I had got myself into.' Robin realised there was little he could do to rein in Tom; instead, he made Adam responsible for his younger brother, which didn't work and only led to the brothers temporarily falling out with each other. 'Robin found all this very difficult,' said his friend and neighbour Anthea Carver, 'but so did Caroline.' Singing with an amateur choir helped her to retain a sense of proportion. Robin and Caroline did have the support of Robin's older children, all three living in London, who were often at the house from the time Adam and Tom were born. Emma would bring books and artists and, said Adam, 'a particular way of thinking about life'. Mark would play the piano or take the boys for walks. Later on, when the boys were teenagers, their older siblings, said Adam, 'were a kind of foil for us'. They did a lot, said Caroline, to help defuse tension. Throughout these trials, the family always remained very close. And there had been good times too, such as visits to the opera and theatre, in particular to RSC productions of Shakespeare at the Barbican.

Once their teenage years were out of the way, the boys settled down and began to see things more clearly; Robin became their friend as well as their father. While he was delighted Adam read English at Oxford, and supported him in his decision to study for the Bar, just as Caroline had, he was less sure at first that Tom would carve out a career in music. But he was always very supportive and as Tom enjoyed success, Robin was, said Tom, 'shocked, amazed and delighted when things started to work out'.

All the children inherited their father's infectious sense of humour. He had, said Tom, 'an utterly cheeky and irreverent and playful sense of humour, and as he became older, it became sillier and more absurd, and we found ourselves able to make one another laugh almost in an instant'. He knew a lot of rude limericks, recalled Emma, and enjoyed making up his own. He would collapse into helpless giggles at a silly joke and carry on laughing until tears were running down his cheeks. 'He made everything fun,' said Adam, 'because, as well as being affectionate, loyal and loving, he was quick-witted and very funny – the best company. He was a relentless tease, although he would show dog-like penitence if he felt he had gone too far. At the same time, his own natural modesty prevented him from ever taking himself at all seriously.'

It was because of his wicked sense of humour, because nothing ever seemed off limits, that it was easy to talk to him and ask his advice. These conversations might develop out of nothing: Robin was always asking questions, always listening to you intently. 'He was always interested to know what was going on in your life,' said his grandson Finn. It was Robin in whom Finn's brother Will confided his plans to go and live for a while in Australia before telling anyone else, even his parents. One of Finn's earliest recollections is his grandfather's 'booming voice and story time when he would read to us, using every different type of accent'. He played football and cricket with them in the garden as he had with his own children. 'Everything we did with him was always fun and there was always an element of naughtiness to it.' Finn's younger brother, Will, was so inspired by Robin that he not only chose to study politics for his degree but also wrote his dissertation on the politics of Ulster.

Although old age, particularly growing deafness, made it difficult for Robin to enjoy the company of his youngest grandchildren, he still made an impression upon them. Several months after Robin's death, Adam's youngest son Otto, aged three, Robin's youngest grandchild, a pupil at Fia's nursery school, was happily painting faces, listing people with blue eyes: 'Otto has blue eyes, Fia has blue eyes, Grandpa has blue eyes.'

With a home in Somerset, Robin was able to see more of his sister Penelope, and there was a lot of affection between them even though they differed over their relationship with their mother. Robin also remained close to his brother James until his death in 2002. Robin and Caroline would travel several times every year to stay with James and Moyra at Moyola, where they always received a very warm welcome. They would see friends or take a picnic into the mountains or onto the moors or visit the nearby country houses and their gardens open to public. They enjoyed walking through the woods around the house, collecting chanterelles from beneath the beech trees in autumn, Moyra frying them in butter on top of the Aga. Robin would fish with James, either on the Moyola or in the west of Ireland, staying in guest houses. On the Moyola, Robin fished for wild brown trout from a boat, rowed by Caroline, in the middle of the river, with Moyra standing on the banks with her dogs, shouting for more fish for supper. Robin also shot with James, firing his last shot on his 75th birthday, the year after his brother's death, with James's gun, the birds on the last drive flying high over the river.

Until the end of his life, Robin's rock was Caroline. 'We were everything to one another,' said Caroline. 'We started a conversation which continued until the last day of his life.' Their devotion to each other was obvious to friends and family. 'Caroline was like balm,' said Jane Manley. 'She looked after him devotedly.' They shared everything from music, literature and art to birdwatching and walking. And there was a lot of singing. The first record Robin gave Caroline was Strauss's *Four Last Songs*, the music that reduced him to tears at the time of Suez. His musical taste was broad, ranging from English and Irish songs and Cole Porter to opera, and he had a fine bass voice, often singing to himself in the house or the car. At Ross House, remembered his son Mark, the collection of classical music had been supplemented by recordings of Bob Dylan, The Kinks, Françoise Hardy and Miriam Makeba as well as *Kiss Me, Kate*, *My Fair Lady* and *Oliver!* Robin loved the Beatles, particularly 'I Want to Hold Your Hand', which he sang with gusto in the car. When he moved into his flat in Wetherby Mews in London in 1971, he sent Mark, staying with him from Eton, to buy a good radio, a record player and a handful of records. 'He was very open to being played new music and I can remember him playing various albums, including *Let It Be*, *Bridge Over Troubled Waters* (which he loved) and Mozart's 40th. He became very keen on Roberta Flack and Carly Simon and would ask to have Dory Previn's "Lemon Haired Ladies" played to him again and again.' Mark also recalled how his father at The Rookery in Yarlington, the weekend before Mark was to marry his fiancée Joanna in the village church, played the trio from the end of *Der Rosenkavalier*, turning up the volume and throwing open the doors of the sitting room. He was trying, he told Mark, to encourage the birds so that they would sing for the happy couple during their reception in the garden.

Robin and Caroline also loved reading, as evidenced by the many shelves in Ellerby Street filled with books on every subject from thrillers to scholarly works. He had a great memory and could quote Shakespeare as well as innumerable poems. They kept an anthology in the car from which they read whenever they were marooned in traffic. As well as visiting art galleries, they were regular theatre-goers, often in the company of friends or family, frequenting the National Theatre, the Barbican, the Riverside, closer to home, and others. 'It was a love affair', said Caroline, 'from the first day until the last. We felt deeply connected on very many levels. Never, ever in all the years we were married did I not want to hear his voice, to see his face, to be with him.'

CHAPTER SEVEN

THE NETWORKER: FROM HEADHUNTER TO FUNDRAISER

After leaving the Commons in February 1974, Robin was out of work for several months. He had no idea what he really wanted to do. Politics was everything he had known since his mid-twenties. He knew that he could not remain for long without some employment. Although he was on the books of several headhunting firms, offers of work he might have accepted never materialised. One major firm, however, Berndtson International, now Odgers Berndtson, was eager not to find a placement for Robin but to employ him directly. The offer came from two of Berndtson's London partners, Tony Whitmee and Kevin Jermey. In the summer of 1974 Robin began his new career as an executive search consultant.

Robin did not intend this to be a permanent position; he hoped something else might come along. But he found that the powers of persuasion he had deployed in politics were equally effective in headhunting. For the next 20 years this was Robin's career. It would be untrue to say that he felt completely fulfilled by his job – much of the work he found dull and he hated commuting into London (latterly on the Tube) – but it did give him great satisfaction to see how people he had persuaded to change jobs could benefit their new employers and how he could build up a good team for companies he respected. And, as his son Mark recalled, Robin 'loved the thrill of the chase'. Moreover, the fact that he was actually good at what he did, earning the respect of those around him, helped to rebuild his confidence, shattered by his experiences during his last few years in politics.

Robin was with Berndtson International only a short while before he joined up with his colleagues Tony and Kevin as partners in forming their own headhunting business. Robin was more comfortable with this more intimate, small-scale operation than the branch office of an international concern. The Welbeck Group, as the new business was called, operated first from Welbeck Street and then from a nondescript office block in Panton Street, off London's Haymarket, the anonymity an advantage in a business where confidentiality was important. While Robin drew his clients from a wide variety of backgrounds, his strength lay in the array of contacts he had cultivated during his time in politics. He was often invited by government departments to find suitable candidates for vacancies on various government bodies. His greatest coup was persuading Sir John King to take over the running of British Airways as the business headed towards privatisation in 1981. Robin's success with John King, a poster boy for Thatcherism, was ironic since he never had much time for Margaret Thatcher. He did admire her courage in her early years as Prime Minister but disliked her abrasive style and knew he would have been regarded by her in political terms as 'a wet'.

Welbeck was eager to make headway in the City. In the early 1980s Robin invited Josslyn Gore-Booth to join him. The Gore-Booth family had been established in Ireland even longer than Robin's ancestors (Sir Arthur Chichester became Governor of Carrickfergus in 1598). They had settled at Lissadell, County Sligo, the country house linked with Constance Gore-Booth, later the Countess Markievicz, famously associated with Irish nationalism and W B Yeats and the first woman to be elected to the House of Commons, although as a Sinn Féin MP she never took her seat. Josslyn had met Robin in 1971 when he spoke on Northern Ireland to the Oxford University Conservative Association, of which Josslyn was president at the time. Josslyn had worked for a number of years in the City before joining another headhunting firm, Carre Orban & Partners. Robin heard Josslyn was looking to move on and invited him for lunch to a very good French restaurant around the corner from the Panton Street office. He explained how the group was trying to expand its business in the City and how Josslyn could help Welbeck to do that.

Josslyn found Robin 'very charming, with a wicked sense of humour'. He was patient and considerate and adept at managing the office staff, which was not always easy. It was, said Josslyn, a very civilised, pleasant and happy working environment. 'It was a genuine partnership', said Josslyn, 'in that there was no primus inter pares, which depended on the considerable personal skills of each of the partners.' It was never a highly profitable business, recalled Alastair Colgrain, who as Alastair Campbell joined the group in 1986, but the partners, he said, were not driven principally by money. Robin, for instance, liked to choose his clients carefully, his selection based on whether or not he would wish to have them to dinner. 'Everything', said Alastair, 'was done in a gentle way but always to make sure there was a good outcome for both the individual and the client concerned.' All three partners were self-effacing, with little interest in self-promotion, and Welbeck was not a well-known name. But Tony, Kevin and Robin were warm, generous and trustworthy, each of them complementing the other, with high standards of integrity. It was run as an equal partnership, the profits divided up amongst the partners, each of them recognising that the firm would have its downs as well as its ups, with the consequent impact on their earnings.

Like Josslyn Gore-Booth, Alastair was invited by Robin to join Welbeck with a view to expanding the group's work in the City. Robin, as usual, was persuasive. 'Why don't you come and give it a go?' was his typical approach. 'Robin', said Alastair, 'was very much my confidante and my mentor in every sense.' In 1986 the City was just adapting to the impact of the Big Bang, which loosened the regulations governing the financial markets. Many people were left looking for new jobs, firms were searching for experienced personnel, and the Welbeck partners were eager to take a share of this new business. Alastair performed well, and the group enlarged its involvement in financial services, but its gentlemanly approach limited its growth in an expanding market. Alastair was eventually approached by a major US firm, Whitney Partners, just setting up in London. He tried to persuade Welbeck's partners to merge the firm into Whitney and almost succeeded before they decided to ditch the idea, largely because they had differing ideas about managing their retirements from the business. Alastair and Robin remained in touch, lunching together every six months or so. 'It was a lovely relationship for me,' recalled Alastair. 'We laughed a lot. I admired him enormously and I valued his judgement.'

When Robin's godson Mark Stroyan was thinking about executive recruitment as a career, Robin shared his own experiences with him. Robin would invite the young Mark to dine with him at Brooks's, where the staff, most of whom Robin knew by name, greeted him warmly, seating Robin and his guest at Robin's usual table. Robin outlined for Mark what he liked and disliked about headhunting: as well as contact with people, he loved the chance it gave him to apply his emotional intelligence, while he disliked the arrogance he occasionally encountered in some clients, which ran counter to his own values. He relished the fact that something he had always enjoyed, engaging interesting people in interesting conversation, was providing him with a living. Robin advised his godson to take a professional qualification first before taking up headhunting on the grounds that it would give him greater credibility. Mark did exactly that, qualifying as a solicitor before embarking on a very successful international career in executive recruitment.

Robin was 66 when he retired. He insisted, recalled his son Adam, that once he had retired, that would be it, he was done with work, he didn't want to do another thing. 'Within weeks', said Adam, 'he was driving everyone crazy.' In fact, Robin already knew what he really wanted to do. In 1988 he had been introduced through a friend to Professor Roy Sanders, a distinguished plastic surgeon, from the Restoration of Appearance and Function Trust (RAFT). This was a medical charity recently set up by Roy Sanders, John Scales, RAFT's first director of research, and Hilary Bailey, together with Roy's colleagues Professor Colin Green, Brian Morgan, Douglas Harrison and Paul Smith. Funds were needed for further research into the treatment of patients who had suffered from severe burns, cancer and trauma. Robin had been suggested to Roy Sanders and John Scales as someone who might be able to help the charity raise the funds it needed to invest in the research it wanted to carry out. Robin was impressed not only by the aims of the charity but also by the commitment of the surgeons involved, who were donating their own fees to RAFT. Robin agreed to help and in 1988 he became the charity's first chairman, holding the position for the next 12 years. At the same time Sir David Napley agreed to act as RAFT's solicitor and Peter Forbes as its accountant.

RAFT was based at Mount Vernon Hospital in Northwood,

Middlesex, which had been established as a plastic surgery and jaw injury centre in 1953. The treatment for most burns patients was to allow the injury to dry by exposing it to the open air. The problem was that for patients suffering extensive burns it was very difficult to dry wounds on any part of the body that remained in contact with their bedding. John Scales, a biomedical engineer, had the idea of devising a bed, based on the same principles as the recently invented hovercraft, which would allow the patient to 'float' above the bedding. With funding from the Medical Research Council, pioneering work by Professor Scales and his colleagues at Mount Vernon would eventually lead to the development of the air mattress technology now in use across the world.

Robin became completely committed to RAFT even in the years prior to his retirement from the Welbeck Group. His involvement, remembered his son Adam, 'brought a gleam to his eye'. He was very happy to use his invaluable network of contacts in aid of the charity, although he had to overcome some initial embarrassment at asking people for money. It didn't take him long to do so, said Adam. 'He became shameless because he realised people wanted to be asked.' But Robin's expertise extended beyond his little black book. He was, said Roy Sanders, an outstanding chairman. He oversaw the appointment of the first board of trustees, kept them all onside and worked well with the charity's first administrator, Hilary Bailey. Among the charity's new trustees was David Pollock, whose PR and marketing agency advised Welbeck; in him, Robin could see not only someone who could help to publicise the charity but also another great networker with a wide range of contacts. Roy was instrumental in obtaining the patronage of the Duchess of Kent as the charity's chief patron. Roy and Robin welcomed her to Mount Vernon in 1993, when she opened the charity's permanent home, the

Leopold Muller Building, named after the principal donor. That donation came about following a fundraising reception for the charity Robin organised at 11, Downing Street, through his wife Caroline, who was friendly with Norman Lamont, the Chancellor of the Exchequer at the time, and his wife Rosemary. Among the guests was Michael Garston, the administrator of the will of Leopold Muller, who was impressed by the plans for the new building which were on display. Roy Sanders had learned about Leopold Muller, who had lost his family in the Holocaust, through a chance conversation while out hunting with David Acland, who revealed he was the sole executor of Muller's will and charged with disbursing every penny of his £20 million estate to good causes. Following the reception, and Michael Garston's favourable report, the Muller estate donated the £750,000 which made the building possible. Among other fundraising events Robin helped to organise were dinners in the White Tower of the Tower of London and at the Mansion House, and a charity performance of Mahler's *Resurrection Symphony* at the Royal Festival Hall.

During Robin's chairmanship, RAFT's research scientists received 32 awards recognising their pioneering work and the charity founded the Institute of Plastic Surgery. As well as the world's first therapeutic air bed, the research funded by RAFT led, for instance, to the development of the surgical techniques and nerve studies which helped sufferers of facial palsy to smile again. For most of Robin's tenure, his deputy was Peter Forbes. Robin, Peter said, although a leader, also believed in teamwork and was always receptive to new ideas. His powers of persuasion, recalled Peter, were invaluable in a crisis. The charity had planned to extend the Muller building, and had raised significant sums to do so, but abandoned the project when it became clear that there was a greater and more immediate need for funds to pay for day-to-day running costs. Robin exercised all his charm to persuade donors to agree to the re-allocation for this purpose of the money they had already given. By the time Robin retired as chairman, the charity was employing 30 people and raising £1.25 million every year.[1]

In the same year, 2000, Robin also gave up his role as chairman of another charity. Arvon had been founded by two poets, John Moat and John Fairfax, in 1968. Their aim was to give writers the time, space and encouragement initially to write poetry, later extended to cover every kind of writing. The charity's name comes from a reference in the *Mabinogion*, the earliest collection of prose stories in British literature. It happened to be the work John Moat was reading when he took a call from the Arts Council. Funding for the charity, they said, had been approved, but could they know its name?

Arvon's first residential course was held in a community centre in Devon, where John and Antoinette Moat were based, for a group of sixth formers from a number of local schools. In 1972 Totleigh Barton, a beautiful thatched farmhouse on the banks of the Torridge in Devon, became the charity's first centre and in the following year Arvon appointed David Pease as its first national director. David held the post for 27 years and made an enormous contribution to Arvon's work. (He would be awarded the Benson Medal for 'conspicuous services to literature' in 2012.) He worked with Ted Hughes to realise the proposal to lease Ted's former home, Lumb Bank, near Hebden Bridge in West Yorkshire, to Arvon as its second centre in 1975. Ted, who later sold the property to Arvon, was the guest speaker on the first course, and he also played a

1 RAFT Appreciation – In Memoriam: Sir Robin Chichester-Clark, https://raft.ac.uk/news/news-in-memoriam-sir-robin-chichester-clark

key part in helping the charity to become a national creative writing organisation. To raise funds for the charity, he initiated the Arvon International Poetry Competition in 1980 when his fellow judges were Charles Causley, Seamus Heaney and Philip Larkin. The winner was another future poet laureate, Andrew Motion.

Robin first became involved with Arvon through one of the sponsors of the poetry competition. Nick Grant, who ran the private bank Duncan Lawrie in Belgravia, was also one of Arvon's council members. He knew Robin and recommended him to David Pease as a person who could be helpful to the organisation. It was then that Robin was invited to the dinner at the Savoy where he sat next to Ted Hughes, whose wife Carol was chair of Arvon. Robin hoped to learn about the life of the Poet Laureate but Ted was intent on finding out details of the life cycle of the dollaghan and they discussed the beauty of names and colours of fishing flies. Soon afterwards, David met Robin, whom he persuaded to become involved. Robin set up the charity's development committee to raise bursary funds, becoming its chairman. In 1997 he succeeded Professor Brian Cox as the chairman of the Arvon Foundation.

As chairman, Robin masterminded the acquisition of the charity's third centre, The Hurst, the former Shropshire home of the late John Osborne, the playwright, in 1999. This brought Robin back in touch with his former colleague at the Department of Employment, Grey Gowrie, who now chaired the Arts Council. One of the other things the two men shared was a passion for literature, especially poetry, Grey himself being a published poet. Grey and his wife Neiti had moved to Wales, close to the border, and knew John and Helen Osborne. Robin and Grey discussed the possibility of Arts Council funding towards the purchase of The Hurst, provided Robin was able to raise matching funding from other sources. There was some doubt among Robin's fellow council members but his enthusiasm for the project was contagious. The Arts Council approved a grant, Robin raised substantial funds from other donors ('Robin', said Grey, 'was a man of action and a very good one') while Grey persuaded a wealthy businessman to make a major donation, and the property was secured for Arvon. In doing so, Robin, said Grey, 'was a very powerful ally since he was so well respected and knew how to play the funding game'. Part of the arrangement was to permit John Osborne's widow Helen to continue to live in part of the large property in return for which she agreed to bequeath the revenues from his estate, effectively his royalties, to Arvon. 'I don't think it would have happened without [Robin's] work on it,' said David. The Hurst became Arvon's largest residential centre.

With Robin's lifelong passion for poetry and literature, he fell in love with Arvon. It was, he would later tell David Pease, the organisation he enjoyed working for more than any other. Robin firmly believed in Arvon's capacity to transform the lives of the writers who attended its courses and both he and Caroline were keen to support through bursaries those who otherwise would have been unable to afford the cost. Robin and David established an immediate rapport: they liked, respected, trusted and understood one another. 'You could not fail to like Robin,' said David, 'but he was a shrewd operator who knew what he wanted and how to get it.' He would lobby council members in advance if there was something in particular he wanted to push through a meeting. On the other hand, although he had presence, he handled meetings so gently that council members usually failed to notice they had been managed. He had, said David, 'more charm than it would be possible to take on board'. He was always available when he was needed, even in the middle of the night, which gave David confidence. As chairman, Robin, in David's opinion, 'imbued Arvon with a new sense of wonderment. He knew best how Arvon should develop and he respected its founding principles. I can't find anything to say against this man'.

Robin's winning charm persuaded many people to support the charity, including several friends, such as Ray Carter, Jane Manley and Alastair Campbell. Jane joined Robin on the newly formed development committee. She was apprehensive at first, uncertain she had anything to offer, but Robin could be very persuasive and eventually Jane would succeed Robin as chair of the committee. Alastair recalled how, shortly before he left Welbeck, 'Robin breezed into the office, saying, "I've got something here that might interest you".' Robin knew of Alastair's love of literature – he had read English at Cambridge – and, with his growing list of City clients, believed he would be an asset for Arvon. Alastair would spend 16 years with Arvon, six of them as a trustee.

Robin, said David Pease, was brilliant at initiating unique fundraising events. The first was a poetry reading at the Duke of York's Theatre, followed by supper at the Garrick Club. Ted Hughes, Seamus Heaney, Diana Rigg and Imogen Stubbs read from the anthology, *The School Bag*. Robin also persuaded Norman Lamont's successor as Chancellor, Ken Clarke, to host another reception at 11, Downing Street, in 1995, assembling an outstanding guest list. 'That', said David, 'was when we knew we were in business with Robin.' There was an outing to Windsor races, where the event included a charity quiz hosted by Bamber Gascoigne, and a further poetry reading at the Duke of York's Theatre, featuring Ralph Fiennes, Andrew Motion, Juliet Stevenson, Imogen Stubbs and Harriet Walter. For the presentation of prizes for a 50-word short story and poetry competition, Robin organised receptions on the Terrace of the Houses of Parliament and in the newly refurbished apartments of the Lord Chancellor.

Robin carried on organising these events after he stepped down as Arvon's chairman in 2000, when he became the charity's life president, an appointment that recognised the huge contribution he had made. Caroline remains a patron. Robin coaxed P D James, one of Arvon's patrons, into writing a short whodunnit. The result was 'Who Killed Sir Richley Luker?', performed for a fundraising dinner at the Park Lane Hotel in 2002. The director was James Cellan-Jones, who persuaded Edward Fox, Joanna David and several other actors to take part. In the following year another poetry reading was held at the Duke of York's Theatre, in aid of Arvon and the Jerwood Foundation, including Harold Pinter, who gave a moving reading of 'Dulce et Decorum Est'. Many of these stars Robin approached indirectly, once again making use of his wide range of contacts, which sometimes meant that he only met them in person in rehearsal. One example was Ralph Fiennes, whom Robin, recalled his son Tom, failed to recognise as the actor took centre stage for a rehearsal at the theatre, asking him, 'So, who have we got here then?'

As well as making a great friend of Ted Hughes, Robin also came to know Seamus Heaney. Coming from the same part of the world, which had shaped both their lives as they were growing up, they had much in common despite their diverse backgrounds. They would debate, for instance, the possible meanings of a phrase such as 'there'll be wigs on the green and hats for the lifting', which Robin's nanny from County Wicklow had often quoted to him.[2] Seamus was thrilled to learn that the middle name of Robin's son Adam was

---

2 The phrase is used now as a ticking off. It is said to come from the Friendly Brothers of Saint Patrick who were set up to stop duelling.

Tamniarn, the name of the red bog where grasses turn red in autumn. It lies beyond the estate wall at Moyola Park, where Robin and his brother James had shot snipe. This, Seamus revealed, was close to his heart, the name of a very secret, very private place.

In his role as president Robin remained an active supporter of Arvon until the end of his life. He was always trying to bring new people into the orbit of the organisation, which he achieved, said Ruth Borthwick, the charity's chief executive, through 'an incredibly soft approach – he was one of the most charming people you could ever meet'. Robin, she said, would leaf through his little black books, trying to match people to the charity's needs. He would phone Ruth and they would arrange to meet to discuss people he had in mind, usually over lunch at an Italian restaurant in Lower Sloane Street. 'Those lunches', she said, 'were always a huge pleasure. Something positive always resulted from meetings with Robin.' They last met at Ellerby Street shortly before Robin's death, where they discussed future fundraising with Arvon's head of development, Robin still thinking which of his contacts it would be most appropriate to approach. Around half-past four, he would offer tea, drinks, and gin and tonics.

For a short period Robin was also involved as a trustee of the Royal Philharmonic Development Trust, serving from 1993 to 1995. (He always took a keen interest in the progress of the Ulster Orchestra and once wrote to David Cameron asking him to consider extra funding for the orchestra at a time when it was in need although nothing came of his request.)

Towards the end of his life, Robin became involved with

Instead of calling someone out for a duel, they would dishonour an opponent by knocking off his hat.

a project suggested to him by his daughter Emma, who had become a well-known illustrator and author of children's books. Emma had been taught by and became friends with Quentin Blake, who was wondering what to do with his archive. Emma suggested it could form the basis of a permanent display of the illustrator's art, which they both felt had been too often overlooked. Quentin, Emma and Linda Kitson, the Falklands War artist and illustrator, first talked about the idea in 2001. One of Emma's friends was Claudia Zeff, whose husband John Brown, the founder of *Viz* magazine, was the son of Sir John 'Bruno' Brown, who all those years ago had once been Robin's employer at the Oxford University Press. Robin had also given the address at Sir John's funeral. Claudia had just left her job as art director of a magazine and Emma asked her if she could help them to develop the idea.

Emma thought her father would make the ideal chairman for the project, given his outstanding track record with RAFT and Arvon, but Robin, who had just given up chairing both those charities, declined on the grounds of age. He did, however, agree to help raise funds. Robin, said Emma, 'loved getting money out of people', but he was also enthused by the project. He persuaded David Pease, who himself had just given up his role with Arvon, to become involved, and David became the first chairman of trustees for what became the House of Illustration. Emma herself was thrilled that her father wanted to take part: 'His being part of the House of Illustration made me feel that he was proud of what I do, that illustration was a worthy cause.'

The first meetings, remembered Claudia, who took on the role of project manager, occurred around Quentin Blake's kitchen table, with Robin in attendance. Robin visited potential donors with Claudia. Initially, Robin suggested he should do all the talking, asking Claudia to be 'light and fluffy'. From anyone else, Claudia said, this would have been offensive but not from Robin, who was equally at home doing what he called 'the fluffy bit' or 'the soft shoe shuffle' when he felt his colleague was up to speed. 'None of us knew what we were doing except for Robin,' said Claudia. His connections once again proved invaluable in opening doors for the project. In these meetings, Robin, recalled Claudia, was 'very self-effacing and immensely charming, but terrier-like'. He would follow up meetings with a charming telephone call or a beautifully drafted letter. 'He was just tireless about it.' Even after he reduced his involvement, he would often ring Claudia if he had found someone he thought could help.

With Robin's help, Claudia registered the project as a charity in 2002, when David Pease agreed to chair the newly formed board of trustees. Another of the founding trustees was one of Robin and Caroline's friends, Anthea Carver. Robin initially courted Anthea with a persuasive telephone call. He knew it would be of interest to Anthea and her husband Jeremy because of the collection of illustrations they had built up over the years. Robin, said Anthea was 'almost deadly charming', and she agreed to join the board, serving for five years from 2003. It was Robin, she said, who was largely responsible for finding all the initial funding. He was unhappy, however, when the trustees, including Anthea, turned down his suggestion for a permanent base for the project at Fulham Palace. He was particularly cross with Anthea, he later told her, although he was never reproachful and always forgiving.

In 2009 Jeremy, a leading international lawyer, also became a trustee. The English, Jeremy noted, are usually hopeless at fundraising, often overcome with embarrassment at asking other people for money. Robin had conquered this reserve many years before when he first became involved with RAFT.

Every approach Robin made, said Jeremy, was carefully considered and clear, which was instrumental in winning commitments from almost everyone he asked. As Jeremy observed, for Robin, gaining funds for any organisation came from creating excellent personal relationships with potential donors, and at this, said Jeremy, Robin was 'an absolute master'.

It took a long time for the House of Illustration to reach fruition. It required persistence and determination and there were plenty of people who thought it would never happen. It was six years before there were any paid staff. With office space generously given by Alan Parker of Brunswick, fundraising could begin in earnest. There were many hurdles to overcome but for Robin it was just one more challenge. 'It was a slog,' said Claudia, 'but Robin was indomitable about it.' And, in the end, it happened, and the UK's only public gallery dedicated solely to illustration and graphic art was opened in Granary Square, King's Cross, in July 2014. Robin had helped to raise some £2 million.

Nigel Pantling, who served as chair of Arvon's board of trustees for nine years, came to know Robin well. He shared with Robin experience of The Troubles in Northern Ireland, having served with British troops in Londonderry and Belfast in the early 1970s. It was Robin's personality, he told the congregation at Robin's memorial service, that made him such a successful fundraiser, 'his humanity, his wit, his natural interest in other people, his unconscious ability to generate trust in the listener, his integrity, his strong belief in social justice … perhaps above all, his ability to get on with everyone regardless of background or circumstance'. 'Robin', continued Nigel, 'had such charm, such warmth and such transparent dedication to his charitable causes that it would have been impossible not to help.' He reminded his listeners of the mixed feelings that came with a phone call from Robin, a mixture of delight and trepidation, trepidation, said Nigel, 'from knowing that before the call was ended, we would have agreed to do something to help one of the charities that Robin loved'. Armed with his impressive list of contacts, Robin had 'a talent for spotting that someone he knew was connected with a grant-giving trust and for devising a pitch for funds perfectly suited to that potential donor'.[3]

---

3 Nigel Pantling, Tribute, RCC's Service of Thanksgiving, 25 Jan 2017

Chapter Eight

IN RETROSPECT

Robin Chichester-Clark died on 5 August 2016. It was nearly half a century since he had relinquished politics. The change, his wife Caroline believed, extended his life. His children, on the other hand, gave Caroline the credit for reinvigorating their father's zest for living. He always retained his love of the outdoors, and liked nothing more than to stride out with his dogs, latterly his springer spaniel Maudie. On his walks he invariably took with him one of the thumbsticks he favoured and if he met someone who took a liking to it, he would happily arrange to have one made for them.

In his later years, however, he suffered several bouts of serious illness. In 2004, he was diagnosed with Hodgkin's lymphoma. As a result of the treatment, he contracted pneumonia, which prevented him from giving the address at the funeral of Caroline's father Anthony Bull on 18 January 2005. The task was handed instead to his son Adam, who would fulfil the same duty at Robin's memorial service. This was a testing time and since Robin was rather squeamish about illness and hospitals and knew little about medicine, Adam took it on himself to help his father by learning as much as he could about his illnesses and getting to know the meaning of the charts hung on the end of his bed. Robin was uncomplaining and enjoyed keeping doctors, nurses and staff entertained.

In the summer of the same year, holidaying on a canal boat in Burgundy, Robin suffered a minor heart attack. Flown by helicopter to hospital in Paris, he was then transferred to the Brompton Hospital in London, where he underwent a triple heart bypass operation. It took him a year to regain his health and his confidence but he was never quite the same again. Nevertheless, he escaped further serious illness until the end of 2015 when he fell seriously ill with a lung infection. 'He managed to keep a smile on his face through dark times,' said his grandson Finn. Robin, said Adam, as things got harder, 'became increasingly open-hearted, sweet-natured and gentle'. And when the clouds seemed darkest, said Adam, 'we would hold hands, quote *King Lear* and laugh together into the storm'.

That year Robin was so ill while spending Christmas at Yarlington that he was treated by paramedics. 'It was nice to be able to hold his hand and to be close to him,' said Finn, 'because he wasn't sure he would make it through that Christmas. He always showed such love, such warmth.' Robin did make it through Christmas and into the New Year but he became increasingly frail as the year progressed. He insisted on travelling to his much-loved North Norfolk for the family's usual summer holiday in August but confided to his son Adam two days before he died that he felt death was not far distant. With Robin largely confined to the cottage, said his son Tom, 'we all talked a lot to him'. Even so, he was relaxed and in good form, found his son Mark, who took his father for what turned out to be his last walk. Robin managed only 400 yards before he and Mark had to turn back. The following day, Friday, Robin was in his dressing gown when Mark called. Robin had already told Caroline he would like to return home early. When Mark said goodbye, telling his father he would see him again that evening, Robin, smiling, held his son's hand and looked into his face, saying, 'Be very, very, very careful.' It was Robin's way of saying how much he loved his son and the last thing he said to him. That afternoon, as Caroline opened the door of the cottage on her return from buying *The Times* in nearby Burnham Market, Robin said to her, 'Thank God you're back. I don't know what's happened. My right leg's not working properly.' As he started to fall, she caught him and he drifted gently to the floor, dying in less than a minute after suffering a fatal stroke.

'My father gave me the feeling I could do what I wanted,' said Emma, Robin's oldest child. 'I always felt he was on my side.' He taught her never to write off anyone and to understand that everyone was approachable. 'He made us think you can trust people to accept you as you are.' 'He gave me a romantic, lyrical way of looking at things,' said Fia, 'and he also helped me to understand by his example how important it is to make those who work alongside you feel as if they really matter. He also gave me my love of dogs!' 'I always knew that he cared deeply about us,' said Mark, 'and he had a way of showing it to us individually to let us know that we were more than just important to him. We knew he would have done anything to help us in any circumstances. His friendship and love were as profound as anyone could wish from a father.' 'I miss his voice a lot, it had such depth and warmth,' said his son Tom. 'I miss our catch-ups and all the stupid nicknames he had for me; I miss talking to him about the state of things; I miss him just as a friend. We all feel we've been really close to him.' He was, said Adam, mercurial and whimsical, hopelessly impractical yet wonderfully inventive, gentle and loving, passionate and inspiring, whose 'heart burned with fire and warmth'.

Caroline was left alone after 42 years of marriage when they had been almost inseparable, rarely spending a night apart. They seldom fell out and if they did, they never let the sun go down on their wrath, as they used to say. Robin was very forgiving, said Caroline, so he was easy to forgive in return. The words Caroline chose from John Donne's 'The Anniversary' for the inside cover of the service sheet for Robin's memorial service underlined their everlasting devotion to one another: 'All other things to their destruction draw, Only our love hath no decay'.

After a service in the small village church, Robin was buried in the churchyard at Yarlington. His headstone bears on the front, his name, dates and the inscription, 'Beloved Husband and Father', while the reverse bears his epitaph, taken from Chaucer, 'He was a true, a perfect, gentle-knight'. A service of thanksgiving for Robin took place five months later on a chilly January day in St James's Church, Piccadilly. Unsurprisingly, the church was filled with people from every aspect of his life, family and friends, politics and charities. Some remembered him as a colleague in the House of Commons where Robin had sat as the Unionist member for the City and County of Londonderry for nearly 20 years. Others were drawn from the charities to which Robin had devoted a large part of his life after politics. That so many filled the church was a testament not just to the contribution Robin had made to public life but to the many friends he had made in doing so. The service intertwined Robin's love of poetry and music with his love of family. Poems by Seamus Heaney ('St Kevin and the Blackbird' – Caroline, alone in the cottage in Norfolk, had heard a recording of Seamus reading the poem on the radio two days after Robin's death, the blackbird being Robin's favourite bird) and W B Yeats ('The Lake Isle of Innisfree') were read by his son Tom and his daughter Emma, while an extract from Chaucer's Prologue to *The Canterbury Tales* was read by his daughter Fia. Mark, Fia and Tom sang a selection of Robin's favourite songs and Mark had composed the blessing which was sung by Robin's grandson Sam. His oldest grandson Finn read the lesson. The music also included 'Beim Schlafengehen' from Strauss's *Four Last Songs*, which Robin had long loved. Tributes were paid by the Duke of Abercorn, Nigel Pantling and Robin's son Adam.

★ ★ ★

Ireland shaped Robin and Ireland almost broke him. The Ireland which he left was a different place from the Ireland into which he had been born. The eternal beauty of the Irish landscape, which influenced Robin so profoundly, had been scarred by violence. The constitutional settlement was broken. The political primacy of Ulster's landed families had almost vanished. Much of what so many had taken for granted and believed would be a perpetual part of their lives had changed. Yet it was clear that this sense of permanency was an illusion, certainly as far as constitutional arrangements were concerned. Why else would so many Unionists spend so much time demonising Irish nationalists and defending partition? But the comparative stability of the first two decades following the end of the Second World War, epitomised by the Brookeborough regime, lulled many Unionists into complacency. All that needed to be done to secure the future of a Unionist Ulster, they believed, was to improve the economic well-being of the population.

At first Robin shared this view but he soon came to realise, along with a handful of others, that this was indeed an illusion. He was eager for the replacement of Brookeborough and enthusiastic about the changes his successor, Terence O'Neill, had in mind. His mistake was to believe that gradual change would satisfy the demands of the minority community in Northern Ireland. It might have been effective had it been adopted by a premier more farsighted than Brookeborough;

by the early 1960s, however, as minorities worldwide were fighting for their civil rights, that moment had passed.

And change was unlikely to be embraced by a Unionist movement which was itself divided. Hardliners like Ian Paisley were exploiting Protestant working class resentment of the landed families who made up the Unionist establishment, a resentment also shared by leading politicians from Ulster's middle class, such as Brian Faulkner. And many of those resentful about the political status quo opposed reform. As a result, Robin and those of a like mind, including his brother James and colleagues such as Stratton Mills, Henry Clark and James Hamilton, found themselves in a difficult situation: gradual reform was too slow for those suffering the greatest discrimination yet completely unacceptable to growing numbers of Unionists. Of these five, James retired to Moyola with a peerage, Henry Clark and James Hamilton lost their seats, and Stratton Mills joined the Alliance Party prior to stepping down from his Belfast seat in 1974, the same year Robin gave up his Londonderry seat, having lost the confidence of his constituency association. The constitutional settlement broke down, severing the long-standing ties between Ulster Unionists and the Conservative party, which had been instrumental in promoting Robin's promising political career. As for the Ulster Unionists, they never regained their dominant position at Westminster and, after mixed fortunes in the intervening General Elections, lost their last two seats in the House of Commons in the 2017 General Election. Although the Belfast Agreement (Good Friday Agreement), which Robin welcomed, brought peace to Northern Ireland in 1998, it cemented the power in Stormont of the DUP and Sinn Féin, leaving little room for the revival of the more moderate politics of Robin and his colleagues. He expressed some scepticism over whether or not power-sharing would work. 'On the one hand, experience, exhaustion and relief from the horrors of daily killings and destruction and perhaps the staggering improvement of the Irish Republic economy may have introduced a unifying ingredient, but on the other hand the marginalising of the middle ground and the banishment of moderates from a place at the helm is a discouraging factor. We can only hope.' In addition, the sensitivity over the border between north and south has never gone away. Recent controversy over the so-called 'backstop', intended to maintain an open border, which has been fundamental to peace in the province, high-lights the continuing ignorance of many politicians on the mainland about Northern Ireland which Robin tried so hard to overcome more than half a century ago.[1]

There was a certain irony that Robin's support of reform, coupled with his principled stand against extremism in Ulster politics, should spell the end for his brand of moderate Union-ism as well as his own future in politics. For Robin, however, his time as an Ulster Unionist MP ultimately destroyed not just his future in politics; it also wrecked his first marriage, damaged his relationship with his three older children and had a serious impact on his mental health. Yet from that experience came the skills that helped him to recover. He redrew his life on a smaller, more intimate canvas, finding greater fulfilment in his involvement with RAFT, Arvon and the House of Illustration than he ever had in politics. His accomplishments in those fields helped to assuage the guilt he harboured for what he saw as his political failure. The latter had in fact opened up a whole new world for him, a loving and lasting second marriage, a new family, the oppor-tunity to develop deeper relations with his older children, a

---

1 Personal Papers, Notes on Maudling and Heath, Mar 2007

wide circle of new friends and many new experiences. It was the story of one man's journey from darkness into light and of a life well lived.

BIBLIOGRAPHY AND SOURCES

Primary Sources

Robin Chichester-Clark Papers, Churchill Archive Centre, Cambridge

Robin Chichester-Clark Personal Papers

The History of Parliament, Oral History Project, Interview of Robin Chichester-Clark: http://www.historyofparliamentonline.org/volume/oral-history/member/chichester-clark-robin-1928

Hansard

Interviews

Abercorn, Duke of, James
Bloomfield, Sir Kenneth
Borthwick, Ruth
Brown, John
Buxton, James
Carter, Ray
Carver, Anthea and Jeremy
Chichester-Clark, Adam
Chichester-Clark, Lady, Caroline
Chichester-Clark, Emma
Chichester-Clark, Mark
Chichester-Clark, Tom
Colgrain, Lord, Alastair
Goddard, Jane
Gore-Booth, Sir, Josslyn
Gowrie, Earl of, Grey
Hobhouse, Penelope
Manley, Jane
Mills, Stratton
Moyola, Lady, Moyra
Pease, David and Tina
Pollock, David and Jane
Pugh, Charles and Tineke
Russell-Cobb, Fia
Russell-Cobb, Finn
Sanders, Roy
Salis, de, Carolyn and Charles

Stroyan, Mark

Stuart-Smith, Sir Murray

Stuart-Smith, Kate

Tebbit, Lord, Norman

Whitley, Edward and Tara

Wiseman, John and Sarah

Zeff, Claudia

Principal Secondary Sources

Bloomfield, Kenneth, *Stormont in Crisis: A Memoir*, Blackstaff Press, Newtownards, 1994

Bloomfield, Kenneth, *A Tragedy of Errors: The Government and Misgovernment of Northern Ireland*, Liverpool University Press, Liverpool, 2007

Campbell, John, *Edward Heath: A Biography*, Pimlico, London, 1993

Faulkner, Brian, *Memoirs of a Statesman*, Weidenfeld & Nicolson, London, 1978

Garnett, Mark and Aitken, Ian, *Splendid! Splendid! The Authorized Biography of Willie Whitelaw*, Jonathan Cape, London, 2003

Heath, Edward, *The Course of My Life: The Autobiography of Edward Heath*, Hodder & Stoughton, London, 1998

Henderson, Deric, and Little, Ivan, eds, *Reporting the Troubles: Journalists tell their stories of the Northern Ireland conflict*, Blackstaff Press, Newtownards, 2018

Hennessy, Thomas, *A History of Northern Ireland 1920–1996*, Palgrave Macmillan, Basingstoke, 1997

Kennedy, Liam and Ollerenshaw, Philip, eds, *An Economic History of Ulster 1820–1939*, Manchester University Press, Manchester, 1985

O'Neill, Terence, *The Autobiography of Terence O'Neill, Prime Minister of Northern Ireland 1963–1969*, Rupert Hart-Davis, London, 1972

Ward, Paul, *Unionism in the United Kingdom, 1918–1974*, Palgrave Macmillan, Basingstoke, 2005

Wills, Clair, *Lovers and Strangers: An Immigrant History of Post-War Britain*, Allen Lane, London, 2017

Wilson, Harold, *The Labour Government 1964–1970: A Personal Record*, Little, Brown, London, 1971

Oxford Dictionary of National Biography

    Brooke, Basil Stanlake, first Viscount Brookeborough (Brian Barton)

    Clark, James Dawson Chichester-, Baron Moyola (C D C Armstrong)

    Craig, William (Bill) (Chris Ryder)

    Faulkner, (Arthur) Brian Adeane, Baron Faulkner of Downpatrick (Henry Patterson)

    Fitt, Gerald Martin (Gerry), Baron Fitt (Chris Ryder)

    O'Neill, Terence Marne, Baron O'Neill of the Maine (Marc Mulholland)

    Parker, Dame Dehra (R A Wilford)

    Paisley, Ian Richard Kyle, Baron Bannside (David C Shiels)

    Redmayne, Martin, first baronet and Baron Redmayne (anon)

Smith, Jeremy, '"Ever Reliable Friends?" The Conservative Party and Ulster Unionism in the Twentieth Century', *The English Historical Review*, 71(490)(2006), pp. 70–103

Jackson, Alvin, '"Tame Tory Hacks?" The Ulster Party at Westminster, 1922–1972', *The Historical Journal*, 54(2) (2011), pp. 453–75

ACKNOWLEDGEMENTS

For anyone writing about the life of someone they have never known, the greatest satisfaction as the last words are written comes from wishing they had, and I certainly wish I had known Robin Chichester-Clark. That I should feel this way about Robin is thanks largely to the recollections of all those people I spoke to who did know him, as a family man and friend, as a politician, businessman and fundraiser. I owe my greatest debt to Robin's family, to his sister Penelope, his sister-in-law Moyra, his niece Tara, his first wife Jane, his children Emma, Mark, Fia, Adam and Tom, his grandson Finn and particularly his second wife Caroline, whose help and hospitality were invaluable. The most interesting period of Robin's life was the time he spent as a Unionist politician in Northern Ireland during a period that straddled the last years of an uneasy peace and the first years of The Troubles. Robin lamented the apathy and ignorance of so many elsewhere in the United Kingdom about the history and politics of Northern Ireland, an apathy and ignorance still evident in the attitude of so many leading UK politicians towards the issue of the border between the United Kingdom and the Republic of Ireland. But it is undeniably complex and my grasp of the issues was immeasurably improved by spending time with Robin's former colleagues as Unionist MPs, James Hamilton, now the Duke of Abercorn, and Stratton Mills, and with the former head of the Northern Ireland Civil Service, Sir Kenneth

Bloomfield. Stratton also gave his time to give me a compressed but helpful tour of Belfast and kindly commented on the draft as did Robin's family. I also enjoyed visiting Robin's birthplace and childhood home, Moyola Park, Castledawson, a stunningly beautiful place, thanks to its current custodians, Edward and Tara Whitley.

There is a large catalogued collection of Robin's papers at the Churchill Archive Centre in Cambridge and my thanks go to senior archivist Andrew Riley and his staff. In addition, Robin's widow Caroline still holds a varied collection of miscellaneous papers.

Nigel Watson
Leyburn, North Yorkshire
May 2019

INDEX

69–70, 74; Robin resolves to stands for 33, 35; Robin stands down 111, 112–13; 1689 siege celebration 5; things come to a head 82; war memorial 72
Long, Walter 4
Lough Erne 55
Lough Neagh 3, 17

M

MacLellan, Brigadier Pat 99
Macmillan, Harold 11, 36, 46, 56
Macmillan, Maurice 103, 112
MacPherson, Hugh 105
Magdalene College, Cambridge 23–6, 68, 119
Maghera 87
Magherafelt 34
Maginnis, Jack 85
maiden aunts 16
Malin Beg 81
Malta 47
Manley, Dickie 127: Jane 126, 127
Mansion House, Dublin 4
Markievicz, Countess 140
Marrakech 110, 120
Mauch, Mitzi 20
Maudling, Reginald 56, 93
McAteer, Eddie 67
McAteer, Hugh 37
McCausland, Colonel Conolly 67, 110
McFarland, Sir Basil 111

McManus, Frank 89
Mills, Stratton: Common Market tactics 51; leaves Ulster Unionists 110; 1922 Committee 48; observing the Apprentice Boys 85; on Robin's dedication 50; O'Neill backed by 63; Robin asks to speak on direct rule 103; tries to combat Protestant extremism 64
Moat, John 146
'Molly' 106
Moore, Henry 57
Morgan, John 129
Motion, Andrew 147
Mount Vernon Hospital, Northwood 143–4
Moyola Park: annual visits 136; building of 4; children of second marriage at 132; cottage in grounds 38; delights of 21; employment of Catholics 7; family home 3; football club 7; Great Hunger queues at 8; hardliners march up avenue to 88; Maudling at 93; nursery 16; requisitioned 23; Robin with Mark at 97; Ted Heath at 54
Muller, Leopold 145

N

'Nanny' 17, 19–20, 150